SON OF CHARLEMAGNE

Also by the Author

Son of Charlemagne

By
BARBARA WILLARD

ILLUSTRATED BY
EMIL WEISS

BETHLEHEM BOOKS · IGNATIUS PRESS
Bathgate   SAN FRANCISCO

Text © 1959, Barbara Willard
Reprinted by permission of Harold Ober Associates, Inc.

Translation of prayer on page 154 by Helen Waddell

Introduction © 1998 Bethlehem Books

Cover design by Davin Carlson
Cover art by Emil Weiss painted by John Herreid

First Bethlehem Books Printing, January 1998

ISBN: 978-1-883937-30-0
Library of Congress catalog number: 97-77061

Bethlehem Books • Ignatius Press
10194 Garfield Street South
Bathgate, ND 58216
www.bethlehembooks.com

Printed in the United States on acid free paper

With love to my godson,
Timothy Marlow—
who will read it
when the time comes,
I hope

Contents

Introduction

TO OPEN THIS book is to break through many layers of what we call Europe—and to stand once again among the foundations. And there we find Charlemagne, who himself is standing on Roman stones. Charles the Great is making a new political beginning which will give shape and sense and spirit to Europe—in some ways right down to our day. Barbara Willard allows us to make acquaintance with this king up close, by way of his children. One great man, willing great good and doing it, and sometimes trespassing hugely—this was Charlemagne, perceived here through the devoted, sometimes pained eyes of Carl, his vigorous young son and namesake.

History shows the indisputable impact of Charlemagne, the only man who succeeded in building an empire in the West in those centuries after Rome fell to the barbarians. Charlemagne's grandsons couldn't keep his edifice; yet there remained for the next thousand years common concepts of justice and a vision of the state in close alliance with the Church. Medieval Europe took shape from those concepts; that vision inspired the Holy Roman Empire, which lasted until 1806. Through hundreds of years when wars, language, and religious quarrels insured a disunited

Europe, Charlemagne's brief realization of a Christian empire remained as backdrop—a fact, an ideal, and a hidden unifying force of immense strength. A Christian empire? That was Charlemagne's dream. His own faults seriously betrayed his ideal at times—once slaughtering thousands of Saxons, in an excessive punishment; imposing the Faith by coercion; manipulating control of power—while meanwhile sometimes subject to the wiles of a woman's power. Charlemagne's own harshness, imposed when he thought it was necessary to obtain rightful ends, fell short of a truly Christian policy—as the renowned scholar and cleric Alcuin and others of his advisors reminded him. Yet despite faults, Charlemagne retained enormous esteem in his day and the centuries that followed as "the King father of Europe."

Son of Charlemagne gives us an intimate view of this man of history, such as will otherwise be known to only a few scholars. Here is a reconstruction for young people that depicts the human, developing life of the man and his sons and daughters. As Barbara Willard points out in her Author's Note, we are introduced not only to a person, but to an entire age, the Carolingian Europe of the 8th and 9th centuries. It is a fully researched picture, in the setting of his day, of the man whose name is attached to the "Carolingian Period." The customs and outward form of that age may be unlike our own. However, the inner struggle of a king's conscience is much like our own—wrestling between Christian standards and the temptation to use brute force, between an ideal of civilization and the solution of imposing it by shortcuts. Touching, exciting, thought-provoking, this book brings an early century back to life.

LYDIA REYNOLDS,
Bethlehem Books

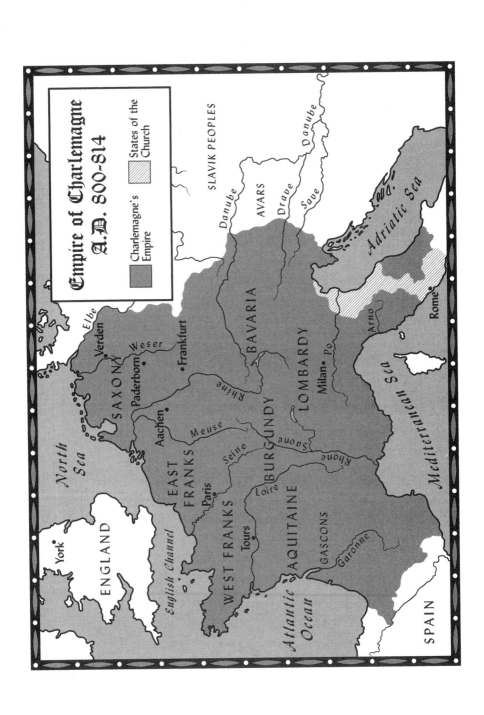

Empire of Charlemagne
A.D. 800-814

Charlemagne's Empire

States of the Church

SLAVIK PEOPLES

Danube

Danube

Drave

AVARS

Save

Adriatic Sea

Elbe

Verden

Weser

SAXONY

Paderborn

Frankfurt

BAVARIA

Rhine

LOMBARDY

Milan

Po

Arno

Rome

North Sea

Aachen

Meuse

Seine

BURGUNDY

Saône

Rhône

Mediterranean Sea

EAST FRANKS

Paris

Loire

York

ENGLAND

English Channel

WEST FRANKS

Tours

AQUITAINE

GASCONS

Garonne

Atlantic Ocean

SPAIN

Author's Note

WHEN YOU READ this book remember that *Charlemagne* is the name given by posterity to more than just one man. Basically, Charlemagne is indeed Charles the Great, Carlus Magnus, Charles le Magnifique. But the legend which grew up around him over the following centuries has come to stand for a whole age, an entire way of life and thought.

You can meet the Charlemagne of legend in the famous *Song of Roland,* the great French epic that was sung by the poetic storytellers of the Middle Ages.

Charles the King, the family man, scholarly and devout, full of little human foibles, comes nearest to us in the *Life of Charles* that was written by the devoted Einhard, while in the *Annals* of the time we learn of his battles and his decrees and so on.

When I call young Carl the *Son of Charlemagne,* I call him also the son of his day and age, when there was almost a new dawn for the Church, and when the seeds of chivalry were sown.

One more thing: there were many minor orders existing within the framework of the Church at that time. To avoid any confusion it is as well to recall that a *cleric* was not necessarily a professed priest or monk, but often just a scholar or *clerk,* employed on the sort of jobs that have occupied clerks ever since.

B.W.

I

Family Journey, A.D. 781

DUSK WAS coming down as the head of the long
train of men and horses and baggage mules
reached the summit of the pass. A strong wind blew
up there, whistling across the roof of Europe, whirl-
ing the sudden snow into blinding spirals that pow-
dered the thick fur cloaks and hoods of the travelers,

lay upon their shoulders, and whitened even their eyelashes. The King's fair beard sparkled where the snowy particles had frozen diamond-hard.

Everyone had dismounted long ago. The horses had to be cajoled along the narrow slippery tracks that were barely tracks at all. Only the mules went blithely; many had had their packs removed because the bulk was too great, and these were being man-handled over this worst section of the mountain jour-ney. There was a great deal of shouting and swearing and praying among the men. But the end of the journey was in sight. Soon they would be dropping down into the plain of Lombardy. The last part of the route would be child's play. By the time the re-turn journey was made flowers would have replaced the snow.

Carl found it difficult to walk, the snow was so deep here at the head of the pass. He would have liked to catch hold of his father's cloak to help himself along, but he was ashamed to appear so babyish. He glanced back over his shoulder, his breath making a thick misty cloud about his head, and saw that his sister Bertha was being carried by Anghilbert; they were laughing and talking together and Bertha's cheeks, whipped by the cold air, shone like apples. Behind them strode the tall Duke Eric, the King's close friend, with Carloman held high against his shoulder. Carl waved to his brother, and young Carloman waved back. There was no sign of Rhotrud, the elder sister. She was probably much farther back, helping their mother with Lewis, the youngest child, who was only three years old. Pepin would be there too; he was the eldest of all, half brother to the rest, but he never managed very well on journeys of this kind.

Just before the summit was reached the King looked back to Carl, who was panting a bit as he plowed along. The tall, striding man paused and held out his hand.

"We'll do better if we give one another a hand, my son," he said, smiling over his frosty beard. "This is enough to tax the strongest of us."

Carl said nothing, but he glanced up gratefully at his father, then clasped his hand in its great fur mitt.

"We shall soon be in shelter," the King said. "Below that great mound of stones the ground drops away and we shall be out of the wind. We will camp there for the night."

Still breathless, young Carl only nodded. He looked toward the pile of stones that reared up out of the snowy twilight, standing harsh and black against the purple sky.

"Look the other way as you pass," his father told Carl. "This is where men once worshiped Jupiter, the pagan god of the ancient Romans. That mound of stones is a place of prayer and sacrifice. One day we will come here in fair weather and scatter the stones and we will raise the Cross in its place."

As they skirted the mighty pile, the King drew Carl within the shelter of his blue cloak, holding its folds against his cheek, as though he would protect his son against an evil which might still linger in that desolate place.

Soon, as the King had promised, they came to shelter. A score of men were there already, knowing the camping ground of old. They were preparing a resting place and they had fires burning. In the increasing dusk the flames leaped comfortingly against the snow. The cold wind, the threatening stone mound, the sinister crags of the mountain's head were left behind. Gradually the whole party assembled. More and more fires sprang into life and the air hummed with the cheerful sound of men busy about making themselves secure against the night. Soon the smell of roasting meat added to the feeling of rest and relaxation.

Against the convenient shelter of rocks six or seven feet high, a tent of skins had been pitched for the King's wife and children; he himself would sleep outside, rolled in his cloak by the fire, a soldier among soldiers. Carl, who had been dodging about among the men and amusing himself with the idea that he, too, was one of them, went at last to find his mother and his brothers and sisters.

"We thought you were lost," his mother said as he strode in and stamped his feet boldly, scattering the snow, so that Rhotrud shrieked and drew aside her skirts. "Come into the warm, my darling. We shall soon have our supper."

It was snug in the tent, with skins on the snowy floor and a brazier by the door. Bertha stood warming her feet and chattering.

"Anghilbert told me a story as we came up the mountain."

"He was lucky to have breath enough—since he

was carrying you!" Carl taunted, and ducked as she kicked off one of the warm slippers she had just pulled on and sent it sailing toward his head.

"About a princess in a tower," Bertha went on, "and how she was rescued by her bold lover. Anghilbert is a wonderful storyteller, Mother."

"We'll ask him for another tale presently," their mother said.

She was busy with the two little boys. She had piled up rugs of fur to make a bed for them. Lewis, the baby, was already asleep. Carloman was protesting against being bundled in beside him, but his mother was firm. On the far side of the tent, the half brother, Pepin, sat and watched the rest. He laughed at Carloman's antics, encouraging him in his disobedience. The child threw off the covers and rushed to Pepin. Rhotrud was after him in a flash. She dragged him back. Her patience was fast going. At last she cried out angrily and slapped Carloman, so that he shouted in fury. Lewis woke and began to cry. Bertha ran to the baby and began to croon over him extravagantly. Carl taunted Carloman for minding what Rhotrud did, and Pepin joined in. Rhotrud, her temper still high, began to cry in her turn.

The din brought the King to the tent.

"Be silent!" he said, standing tall and stern in the opening.

And they were silent, even Lewis, the baby.

"Are these my children?" the King demanded. "Or a pack of wolves?"

Their mother laughed and held out her hand to

the King. His sternness left him as he went toward her.

"Hildegarde," he said, shaking his fist at her, "have you no care that your sons and daughters behave like wild animals?"

"You bring them to forage in the snow," she told him, still laughing. "They are certain to grow a little like the creatures who live in these wild places. If you prefer a tame and docile family you must leave us all behind in the palace at Aachen. I daresay we should behave ourselves better there."

"No," he said, his arm firm about her shoulders, "I shall always take my pack with me and accept the consequences. Snapping and snarling are better than separation."

"Be thankful you have a wife who is not too dainty to tramp over the mountains with you, my dear," Hildegarde said. She took his hand and held it for a moment against her cheek.

"I am thankful," he assured her seriously. "I praise God seven times a day for my Hildegarde."

At that moment the servants came in with food and wine. The family gathered round thankfully, for the cold air and the long day's journey had given them sharp appetites. Lewis sank off to sleep again, and the King took Carloman on his lap and fed him the choicest bits of meat. The other children looked a little resentful at this favoritism, but their mother watched with a soft and contented expression. This was one of the moments she most enjoyed, when her husband forgot all the cares of his kingdom and settled down with his growing family as easily as any peasant. Charles, King of the Franks, was a great warrior, a great ruler, a great scholar, a great Christian; but it was by his simplicity that Hildegarde his wife knew him to be a great man.

King Charles of the Franks was on his way to Rome. This was no military expedition, such as he had conducted for many years throughout Europe, where man was at last emerging from the dreadful night of the Dark Ages. When the Roman Empire collapsed, much of Europe slipped back into savagery and paganism. Christianity had seemed almost on the point of extinction. But in the lonely and often threatened monasteries, the monks diligently working kept a little flame of faith and learning burning steadily. Gradually the darkness lifted. And Charles of the Franks was the champion who had arisen to reawaken and restore the Church, and order in civil things, and the precious knowledge of books and the things of the mind. They had called his grandfather Charles the Hammer because of his strength and indomitable power. He it was who had founded the new line of Christian kings of whom the Frankish King Charles was the greatest yet. The greatest man, some said, who had ever ruled an earthly kingdom.

Charles of the Franks, successor and soon superior of his powerful grandfather, had thrust his way about Europe subduing race after savage race, converting them to Christianity and making them his vassals. Yearly his kingdom grew wider and more

powerful, stretching from the Pyrenees toward the
Baltic shore, reaching out to the Breton frontiers and
the Netherlands or Frisia, and over the great Alps into
Lombardy. The Saxons, under their leader Witikind,
had fought the most fiercely against King Charles.
They were not yet subdued, but they were quiet; and
Witikind had fled into Scandinavia. So, in a period
of apparent peace, the King was on his way to visit
the good and noble Pope Hadrian in Rome.

King Charles had more than one reason for this
journey. Ostensibly he wished to visit those lands of
Lombardy which had come under his rule only a few
years previously. He wished to present his sons to the
Pope. But most of all he intended the visit to be a
preparation for the future—a future whose ultimate
aim was so great and grand he had barely dared to
put it into thoughts, let alone words.

"Save me, O Lord, from my own arrogance!" was
a prayer the King spoke often and often. Then he
would add: "But strengthen me in arrogance for Thy
sake!"

Although there was still a Roman Emperor, his
throne was no longer in Rome but in Constantinople.
He was a minor under the control of his mother, the
Empress Irene. In his secret heart, Charles dreamed
of a new Roman Empire, one based and rooted firmly
in the Christian faith, as the old Empire had been
founded on paganism. By appearing in Rome now,
with his counselors and his warriors and his sons,
he meant to lay such foundations as must inevitably
work not only for his own good but for the good

of Christian Europe. To do so he must make a personal sacrifice which so far he had confided to no one.

The night which had settled over the encampment in the mountains was clear and cold. The wind had dropped and the stars were now so thickly sprinkled it was difficult to see a pin's space between them. Circling the sleeping men were the fires carefully tended by the guards, a protection against wolves and bears, and perhaps some would say against those evil spirits which might still linger on the mountain side. The King looked over his encampment and felt some satisfaction that the journey had gone well so far. He would never allow himself to be beaten by the difficulties of travel at a time when only the roughest routes led over the foothills and the passes of the mighty Alps. Some losses were inevitable. Three horses had plunged over a precipice on the fourth day; two days after that a suddenly displaced boulder had caused the death of two men. Otherwise everything had been smooth enough, a compliment to the organization of a hardened campaigner who could rely utterly on his followers.

The King smiled as he thought of those followers, soldiers and servants, friends and statesmen and scholars, who went with him unquestioning, that his administration might be maintained even though he were away from home for months. And with them went Queen Hildegarde, cheerful and loving and unflurried by hardship, caring as splendidly for the children as if she were safe in some city palace.

The thought of his wife led the King to consider

his sons. He began to pace quietly in the snow, trying to assure himself that what he was about to do was the right thing, praying that he might not be making a mistake in so laying his plans that this happy family must be broken and scattered. How would he soothe the grief of Hildegarde when she knew his intention? Would she ever forgive him for thinking so much of the future that he was prepared to sacrifice the contentment of the present?

Drawing his cloak tighter about him, the King sighed. He moved toward the tent where his family lay sleeping. For a moment he felt he must enter and awaken his wife, and so end his loneliness. But he hesitated to burden her before he needed to. So he passed on, with his problem and his decision still heavy about him.

The sound of the King's footsteps in the crunching snow roused Carl. He, too, rolled himself tighter in his cloak. Wanting to emulate his father in all things, he had scorned the soft bed of furs and settled himself down by the fire. But the ground felt cold and hard and it was difficult to sleep deeply.

Carl pulled back a corner of the tent flap very gently and saw his father's tall figure pass, sharp against the starry sky. The boy rose, shivered a little as the cold air struck him, and stepped outside.

The guard standing a pace or two away turned his head at once. He grinned when he saw Carl, but barred his way none the less.

"You will have me in trouble, young sir. Where are you going at this hour?"

"Let me pass, Wolfred," Carl said, pushing aside the spear. "I cannot sleep. I am going to my father."

"Then tell the King I would have stopped you if I could."

"I'll tell him," Carl promised.

When Carl reached his father, the King had paused by a fireside. He was holding his hands out to the glow, and the guard had retired a few paces that his master might be alone.

"I can't sleep either," Carl said, rubbing his hands in his turn.

"Stay with me a little then. What keeps you awake? You have no worries, at your age."

"Are you worried, Father?" Carl asked, surprised, for he could not imagine that his father ever had doubts of anything at all. "Is it because of the difficult journey? Will it be worse tomorrow?"

The King shook his head. He took Carl's hand and held it firmly. "When we come to Rome you will know that I am naming you my heir. One day you will rule over all my lands. I want you to remember that I trust you to continue the work I have begun."

Carl frowned. "But, Father . . ."

"I know what you are going to say. You are not the eldest. There is Pepin. Pepin, whose mother was my first wife. Pepin, whose name—" He broke off and sighed deeply. "What is it the men call the King's eldest son, Carl?"

"They call him Gobbo. We all do, Father!"

"You do not know what it means?"

Carl hesitated. He knew but did not want to admit the fact. He knew too there was a certain amount of contempt for his half brother among the court and army. And he was a difficult boy. Hildegarde always took pains to treat him gently as if he were her own, but he remained aloof. He was the most handsome of the whole handsome family, save for one thing.

"Gobbo means hunchback," the King said. His voice was bitter. "The men picked the word up in Italy, when we fought the Lombards the year you were born. When I heard my son called Gobbo I knew he must not succeed me. No King must be mocked. Besides—"

He paused, and Carl peered into his face, waiting.

"Besides—what, Father?"

"Remember this, Carl—it is a warning. I fear that Gobbo is not entirely to be trusted."

As his father spoke, Carl remembered that Gobbo was indeed inclined to spiteful tricks. He knew, though, that this was because he was often left out and thrust aside. Carl realized that if Gobbo had to fight back to make up for his misfortune, it was because of the unkindness of those who should, rather, have helped him. He flushed in the dark to realize that he himself had often enough pushed the elder boy out of the way, and taken advantage of running faster, fighting harder, never feeling tired or sickly.

Carl had heard the King called stern and implacable, but no man had ever questioned his wisdom. Now his face in the starlight was so full of pain that

Carl could hardly bear to look at it. Vaguely he knew that what his father intended doing would always seem cruel, and that the King himself knew this but would act according to his own honest certainty of what was right for the future of his kingdom and thus for Europe and all Christendom.

"You are young," his father said, as though he read the boy's thoughts. "But you must try with all your might to understand. He is my son and will always be dear to me, as all my children are. But I have made my decision and I will abide by it. You are my heir."

"Does he know?" Carl asked.

"No. You will not speak of it to him or to anyone. Get back to sleep now. I will see the guards changed and then I shall sleep, too. God be with you, child."

"And with you, Father."

Carl went back through the snow to the tent and crept inside. The brazier was glowing and in its light he saw his brother Gobbo leaning on one elbow. The rosy light painted his shadow hugely on the wall of the tent.

"I saw you with him out there," Gobbo said, in a sharp low voice. "You sneak after him, trying to win favors."

"Leave me alone, Gobbo," Carl replied. He used the nickname without thinking. Immediately the word was out he bit his lip and flushed. "Can't you sleep?" he asked gently, anxious to make up in some way for his half brother's misfortune.

"I am too tired, Carl. It was heavy going over the

pass." He shivered. "I keep thinking how those men were killed—and the horses . . ."

Carl drew near and slipped in under the skins beside the elder boy, wanting to comfort him, drawing the furs up until they tickled his chin.

"If we huddle together we'll soon be warm. We'll soon sleep. It's so starry outside it's like day. Wolfred was on guard, but now they're changing. Wolfrith, his twin brother, will take his place. Do you wish," Carl asked, "that we were twins?"

"Should I be like you—or you like me?"

There seemed no easy reply to that. Carl closed his eyes and settled down. Much later he awoke once more. The brazier had been tended by the guard. Its glow showed Carl the sleeping heaps that were his mother and his sisters and brothers. It showed him, too, the unsleeping Gobbo, his eyes wide open and brimful of tears; he was biting his knuckles as though his sorrow and loneliness were too much for him to bear.

II

The Palace School

IN LOMBARDY they were all housed in a ducal
palace. Their struggle across the mountains at once
seemed very far away, for here the spring was very
soft on the air, the poplar trees were shaking out
leaves so tender and young they were gold rather

15

than green. It was possible to walk out in the sun without a cloak.

For Carl, for all the family but the two little boys, Carloman and Lewis, the comfortable lodging meant that school must start again. For just as the King took with him abroad his counselors and captains, so, too, he took with him tutors and clerks. Wherever the King's court was established, there too was established the palace school, where his sons and daughters, and the sons and daughters of his friends and followers, down to the humblest, sat side by side to learn what wise men could teach them. And sometimes the King himself came to school.

"I'd rather be a hunter or soldier," Carl complained, "than a silly scholar."

"Father must not hear you say so," Rhotrud warned. She was a rather severe little girl and liked to keep her brothers in their place. "You know he will have us all scholars before we can be anything."

"It's all right for you and Bertha," Carl said. "You will never be soldiers. The best you can do is to marry kings."

"I shall marry Anghilbert," Bertha declared.

She was a fair-haired sturdy child, very like the King in features—Carl's particular friend who would always stand up for him and expected him to do the same for her.

"Anghilbert is no king!" Rhotrud cried. "He's nothing but a poor clerk."

"He is a scholar!" replied Bertha. "So he must be a splendid person."

At that moment Anghilbert came into the room where they were sitting, and Bertha turned scarlet.

"Lesson time," Anghilbert told them. "We are to go to the far hall, and the King will join us there. Hurry, then, and take your places."

"Will you tell us a tale, Anghilbert?" Bertha asked, running beside him along the stone cloister that led to the King's quarters, and skipping every now and again in an attempt to keep up with his long stride.

"Master Peter is to talk of mathematics," he replied. "And there is a Lombardy scholar come to tell us his findings in astronomy. After supper, Lady Bertha."

"About the lady in the high golden tower . . . ?"

"No!" Carl broke in. "About Roland. Tell us again about Roland, Anghilbert. And Oliver. And the Twelve Peers. And the horn. And the sword Durandel."

Anghilbert looked quickly over his shoulder and frowned.

"When we are private. Do not let your father hear the name Roland. You know he will never speak of that day of defeat."

When the King was campaigning against the infidel Saracens, who had long occupied Spain and threatened all Europe, the flower of his following had been trapped and slain in the long defile of Roncesvalles in the Pyrenees. Young Roland had been there, the Warden of the Breton Marches, of whom great things had been hoped, whose deeds in the field were already spoken of with admiration. Treachery had caused the death of those splendid warriors, but Charles the King always blamed his own faulty generalship. Even now he would cover his face and weep when the names of Roland and the rest were spoken in his presence. And so those about him guarded their tongues and when the tale was told, a tale of proud and desperate valor in the face of fearful odds, it was told secretly. . . .

As they reached the hall, where the school was to be set up, they heard a great babble of voices. The children of the duke whose palace they lived in had come to join the school, and with them the children of the duke's servants, his huntsmen and stewards. And there were many other strangers, grown men anxious to benefit from the opportunity offered by the presence in Lombardy of the King of the Franks. There were several monks there, and some quite rough fellows, and a richly clad, portly man who must have been a merchant. When the King's children came in, these strangers rose out of respect. But Anghilbert called to them at once to be seated.

"In this school learning is our king and all pupils are equal in the eyes of their master."

Anghilbert himself was in charge of the class that morning. He was a splendid teacher. Even Carl, who had come reluctantly to his lessons, fell under the spell of Anghilbert's voice and manner, and the way his eyes flashed with enthusiasm as he spoke to them of what man knew of the world in which he lived.

Anghilbert cut short his own discourse to allow Master Peter, the monk, to instruct them in mathematics. Immediately Carl's attention flagged. Master

Peter spoke through his nose, and he had a sharp, rather angry manner which softened only when he spoke to Rhotrud, who was his favorite pupil. Rhotrud knew this perfectly well and made the most of the situation. She had a clear, eager mind, astonishingly agile for her years; she was the only one of them all who really appreciated Master Peter's calculations.

As for Bertha, she paid no attention at all to Master Peter, but sat watching Anghilbert, who had taken a place a little behind the speaker. He sat leaning forward with his elbow on his knee and his chin on his fist. He had a lean, clear-skinned face and dark eyes that sparkled with humor. The sun shone through the high archway at his back. He wore a red mantle over his dark green tunic, and the color glowed warm and rich in the sunshine. Once he looked across to Bertha and smiled. But although she was his favorite pupil, just as Rhotrud was Master Peter's, he never neglected his other pupils for her sake, as Master Peter did. As he was doing at this very moment, taking so long to discuss the problem with Rhotrud that the rest of the class began to fidget and whisper.

Carl glanced at Anghilbert to see how he was taking this. Anghilbert's face told him nothing, but under the hem of his tunic his sandaled foot tapped on the stone floor. He shifted his position and leaned back against a pillar, folding his arms. Carl felt a glow of admiration as he watched. Anghilbert was one of the people he liked best in the world; he was wise and knew how to teach his wisdom, but he was merry too, and he wrote songs that he sang in a fine voice,

strong and yet tender. Some of the songs were stirring, about battles in lonely places and horsemen
spurring under the full moon across trackless plains;
some were songs of love and romance; and some
were songs of prayer that you might remember if
you woke in the dark night, speaking over the words
softly and sleeping again in comfort.

Everyone but Rhotrud and Master Peter was beginning to yawn. Carl looked out through the archway
to the courtyard beyond. He saw his father crossing by
the fountain with a stranger at his side. Carl saw no
more than that the stranger wore the sober clothes of
a clerk, that he was tall and walked proudly. Then the
two men moved out of sight into the shadow of the
cloister.

But the King's page had run ahead and came into
the hall where the school was assembled.

"Master Anghilbert," he cried in a loud voice. "The
King is coming. With him a visitor from overseas."

"What visitor, page?"

"It is Alcuin of England!" the boy replied.

A quick excited murmur at once arose. Master Peter forgot even Rhotrud. The name of Alcuin was
known and respected by many of the older students
present. The Englishman was spoken of as the spiritual heir of the great scholar Bede of Yarrow, whose
missionary work was recognized wherever the Christian faith had found root.

Alcuin had been in Rome to take council with the
Pope on behalf of the Archbishop of York. Now on
his way home to England he had paused in Lom-

bardy to make himself known to the great King of the Franks. Alcuin was not the only man of God who realized that King Charles held in his hands the whole future of the Christian world. Perhaps he had come to find out exactly what manner of man this King was so that he might carry the tidings home with him. And perhaps he had approached the meeting with reserve, with even a little suspicion. For the name of Charles of the Franks was ringing round all Europe in these days of change and stress, and it might well be that a cautious man would feel inclined to suspect so great a volume of enthusiasm.

However that might be, Alcuin was there in the ducal palace, and he and the King were approaching together toward the school. As they entered the hall and the students surged to their feet in eager greeting, Carl looked swiftly from his father's face to that of the stranger. He could not have explained what made him believe then so joyfully that his father had met a man who would forever be his friend; and that Alcuin knew this and was glad.

Alcuin was tall and upright—quite as upright, nearly as tall as the King. But it was the stern gentleness of his eyes and the shape of his mouth, firm yet ready to smile, that most pleased Carl.

He saw his father looking at him. "Carl—come here and greet Master Alcuin for us all."

Carl stepped out into the front of the class. He gave a quick grin at the stranger, then screwed up his eyes as though he would take a mental look at all the Latin words he knew and thus be able to decide which were best to use on this occasion. Suddenly he was nervous and tongue-tied and knew he could not find the words he needed.

"We are all waiting, boy," the King said; and Carl thought he sounded disappointed in his son.

Carl glanced frantically round the class, at the students young and old, strange and familiar, waiting to hear what he would say to Alcuin in greeting from them all. Then he caught sight of his half brother, sitting over in the far corner. Gobbo was staring intently at Carl, he was willing Carl to look that way and to understand what he wanted. Gobbo knew what to say and was begging for the chance to say it.

For what seemed to Carl ages of time, the silence held while he tried to make up his mind what to do—to admit his own failure and give Gobbo his chance, or at least to make an attempt, however bungling.

"Well, never mind," the King said. He laughed a little. "He is very young."

"My brother, sir—" Carl stammered.

But it was too late.

"Anghilbert," said the King, "I see how eager you are for this opportunity."

Eager indeed to greet a man of whom he knew so much, and all of it good, Anghilbert stepped forward swiftly and clasped Alcuin's hand. Always fluent, he now surpassed himself in the graceful honesty with which he welcomed the visitor. An appreciative murmur ran over the class.

Carl went back slowly to his place. He could not

look at Gobbo, and his self-disappointment made him sullen. He was aware of his two sisters watching him; Rhotrud impatient with his stupidity, Bertha sympathetic. The younger girl moved to his side and slid her fingers into his. But he jerked his hand away, too cross with himself to accept her friendly gesture.

"I have brought Alcuin here to our school," the King was saying, "that he may judge for himself of our industry and desire for learning. I would I might persuade him to stay with us, to be head teacher of the school, master over all of us—yes, Anghilbert, master over you too."

"It is too fine a dream," Anghilbert replied. "What a school we might have then—and what scholars we would make!"

Then the King invited Alcuin to take the master's seat and speak to the class of what he chose, whether of his own country, or of historical matters, or of poetry and religion.

"I will speak of Bede," said Alcuin, "the greatest man our monastery has known. In the year that I was born, he died. I would I had come to this world sooner, that I might have been his pupil—one of those, perhaps, to whom he dictated his translation of the Holy Gospel of St. John. But you all know that story."

Some of them knew and others not. The King begged his visitor to tell the tale again.

"The great scholar knew that he was near his death," Alcuin said. "Each day his pupils gathered about him as he lay on his bed, weak in flesh but strong and bold in spirit, striving still that he might finish the work that was dearest to his heart. Soon almost all the great Gospel was committed to parchment, and soon the Abbot would be able to rest.

"It came to the Festival of the Ascension of Our Lord, and away went all the young scholars to keep the feast. Only one scribe remained that day with Abbot Bede.

" 'Dearest Master,' said the scribe, 'there is yet one chapter wanting, and it is hard for thee to question thyself.'

" 'No, it is easy,' said the Bede, though his breath was shallow and his heart beat heavily against the frail wall of his breast. 'Take thy pen and write quickly.'

"So all day they worked together, the old man and the young. Then it was evening and the boy saw that his master grew weaker every moment.

" 'There is yet one more sentence, dear master, to write out,' said he.

"The Bede smiled and said in his frailest voice: 'Write quickly!'

"So the quill flew over the parchment and at last the old man's voice was silent and at last the pen stopped on the final word.

" 'Now it is finished,' said the boy in the silence.

" 'Well, thou hast spoken truly,' said the Bede. 'It is finished!'

"Then the boy called the returned brethren, and the great scholar bade them place him where he could look on the spot where he was wont to pray. And he began to chant the *Gloria.* But as he uttered the words 'the Holy Ghost,' he breathed his last.

"And so on that day," said Alcuin, "the Feast of the Ascension, the twenty-sixth of May in the year of Our Lord 735, the great Bede, his work accomplished, died and passed to the Kingdom of Heaven."

A deep silence followed Alcuin's soft and steady voice. As soldiers will feel their hearts beat harder at a tale of battle and heroism, so these scholars, whose eyes looked to a great future, felt a surge of spirit and inspiration as they recalled the tale they had just been told.

Then the King rose. Swiftly the students followed him. With one thought and one great voice they began to chant as the dying Bede had chanted:

"*Gloria in excelsis Deo, et in terra pax hominibus bonae voluntatis. . . .*"

III

Kings in the Making

WHILE THEY rested in Lombardy the spring came to its full splendor, and the day they approached Rome the sun shone brightly, the air seemed full of promise. All along the ranks of King Charles's following, excitement ran like a delightful breeze. They were coming to the Eternal City. They would see the Pope himself, the Holy Father, the head of the Church, St. Peter's deputy, whose hands now held the crozier and the keys that were the sacred symbols of his great office.

At the head of the column the King rode with Hildegarde at his right side. On his left Duke Eric rode, and behind came a good company of counts—Edo was there, and Roccolf and Hildigern, Udolf and others. Carl and Gobbo were side by side after the counts, with Anghilbert, and with Arnold, who held a trusted position in the royal household. After them came the rest of the family, Rhotrud and Bertha on white palfreys, and the two youngest children, Carloman and Lewis, in the care of their nurses and stewards. What with the soldiery and the servants and the baggage mules and the spare horses, the train stretched away along the road in such size and splendor that men and women ran from their homes as it passed to stare in amazement and awe.

They were still a mile or two from the city when the King held up his hand and the train came to a straggling halt.

"What's the matter?" Carl wondered. "Can you see anything, Gobbo?"

"There's a band of horse coming along the road toward us," Gobbo replied. He had immensely long sight, the others would always ask him to report on what was ahead, wherever they might be. "Yes, look, Carl—there's dust rising!"

"Will they be bandits?" Bertha asked, sounding

more excited than alarmed. "Shall we skirmish with them?"

"They're riding slowly," Gobbo reported. "It is quite a small cloud of dust."

"The Pope must have sent an escort to lead the King into the city!" Rhotrud cried.

The present feeling of excited anticipation increased as word of the approaching riders ran back along the column. The King now beckoned them on. This time they rode slowly, talking together in loud eager tones. The long journey was nearing its end as the two parties of riders approached one another along the sunny road leading across the plain to the hills and the splendors of Rome.

Suddenly the King threw up his hand and reined in his horse so abruptly that those following behind were thrown into confusion. There was a ringing of hoofs on the dry road and a shouting of men to their beasts.

"The King has dismounted!" Gobbo cried.

The King, afoot in the roadway, had pushed back the hood he was wearing and now stood bareheaded, facing the oncoming riders.

Duke Eric shouted something over his shoulder; then he, too, dismounted and holding out his hands to Hildegarde, helped her from the saddle. Grooms ran up to hold the horses.

The word that Duke Eric had tossed over his shoulder like a golden coin was seized and handed back, was called and shouted in increasing triumph and awe.

"It is Pope Hadrian! It is the Pope himself who

comes to greet our master. God save His Holiness! God bless his days! May his reign be long! God bless Pope Hadrian, our Holy Father! God be with St. Peter's heir!"

And as the cries of greeting and blessing swelled and rang over the great column brought to a standstill there in the open plain, the bareheaded King knelt in the dust, waiting for Pope Hadrian to approach nearer and receive his homage.

Hadrian had himself dismounted. He came now toward the King, holding out his arms, his face full of the warm affection he felt for this great man who was yet ready to bend his head and his knee when occasion demanded. Hadrian placed his hands on King Charles's shoulders and embraced him warmly.

"Welcome, my son! Welcome to this great and holy city! May God bless you and keep you! Rise up, my good friend Charles, and let me lead you home."

Bertha murmured to Carl in astonishment: "He is an ordinary man!"

"What did you expect him to be?"

"A sort of archangel, I suppose."

"Yes—with a halo and long golden wings," Rhotrud agreed, not bothering to appear clever for once. "But he has the face of a very kind man. Much less frightening than an archangel."

"Of course he is an ordinary man!" Gobbo said, sneering a little. "And just as ambitious and cunning, I daresay, as any other mighty ruler."

"Peace, Gobbo!" Anghilbert cried sharply.

Gobbo flushed. "You call me by my nickname. Call

me Pepin—call me Lord Pepin. I am your master's eldest son!"

Anghilbert looked away. "You must forgive me," he said. But whether for using the name Gobbo or for failing to use any other was not clear.

Hildegarde was standing close to her husband, his arm was about her shoulders. He was presenting her to the Pope, and she sank to the ground in a low obeisance. Again came Hadrian's warm and gentle smile as he blessed her and then held out his hand for her to kiss.

Then the King and the Pope turned gladly to one another, breaking into eager conversation, the conversation of friends who have not met for a long time and have much to say to one another. The King looked back over his shoulder and called a name.

"He wants us," Carl said to Bertha, taking her hand.

"No—he is calling you, Carl." She gave him a push. "Go along quickly."

As Carl moved forward uncertainly, knowing his father's eye was upon him, Gobbo moved too. The two boys jostled momentarily. Then the King called again: "Carl!"

Gobbo fell back at once. Not daring to look at him, Carl hurried forward and in his turn he dropped on his knees to receive the blessing of the Pope.

It was dark in the chapel and it seemed to Carl that he had already been there a very long time. The floor was hard and cold. He wished he had soft long skirts to kneel on, like his sisters. Rhotrud had her face hidden in her hands and seemed very comfortable; she always prayed longer and more devoutly than any of them. Sometimes Carl found this rather trying. He was forever peering sideways to see if she had finished yet, wondering how in the world she managed to find so many words. Carl's prayers, those that he made up for himself, were short and to the point: Lord, let me remember the answers in school. Good Lord, grant me a new hunting knife. Lady Mary, intercede for my hawk that she may beat Gobbo's and all the others, too. . . . As for Bertha, she had an enviable way of looking smooth and contented when she said her prayers.

The chapel was full. Duke Eric and the counts were there; so was Anghilbert, so was Arnold; and with them many nobles and many church dignitaries of Rome. Hildegarde sat in a chair with a purple cushion, Lewis on her knee, Carloman perched on a velvet stool at her feet. Carloman was admirably quiet and no one seemed to notice that he was amusing himself by picking threads out of the embroidered hem of his mother's skirt.

The King had not yet arrived, nor the Pope. A slight restlessness became apparent among those who waited. The ceremony was already the better part of an hour late in starting.

Carl thought it strange that Lewis and Carloman were to be christened here in Rome. They had of course been baptized at birth. Now for some reason the boy did not understand it was all to do again.

"Will they get new names?" Carl whispered to

Bertha. "What would you choose, if you could have a new one?"

Before she could reply, the Pope and King Charles entered by the door behind the altar and moved down toward the crowd assembled near the baptismal font. A sharp attentive stillness then fell upon the throng. Then the rustling and the fidgeting which had been stilled after the congregation rose broke out again on the softest hint of a whisper. The Pope and the King were late because they had been conferring privately; it was difficult not to feel that they had been arguing a matter of great importance, that the delay was caused by a clash of wills. As they entered the chapel side by side, none could tell which of the two men had had his way.

The King smiled at his wife. He nodded his head, and as though this was a signal prearranged between them, Hildegarde rose, holding the three-year-old Lewis by the hand.

"Bring the child to me," the Pope said.

Hildegarde gave Lewis a little push and he went toward the font in an uncertain, wondering way, pausing to turn and look up at her once, waiting for some sign of encouragement. His mother smiled and nodded to him, and the child moved forward. When he stood by the font the top of his head was nowhere near the rim. Pope Hadrian at once put his hands on Lewis's head and blessed him. Then he held out his hands to the nearest acolyte, who turned back his fine lace-trimmed sleeves so that his wrists were bare and he could the better dip his hand into the font.

"It doesn't take long, does it?" Carl asked Bertha.

"It doesn't at home," Bertha replied, with a memory of large numbers of heathen, enemies until the King subdued them, bowing their heads and receiving this sacrament which made them members of the Church they had till then defied.

It was true that the actual christening was soon over. But as Hildegarde put out her hand to draw Lewis back to her side, the Pope restrained her.

"Let the boy stay beside me. Where is his brother?"

Hildegarde looked at her husband in surprise. Carloman was now a little more than four. Was he, too, to be rechristened?

Carl and Bertha exchanged a rather uneasy glance. Even Rhotrud flushed a little. Were they all to go through the ceremony? If so, their father should have warned them that they were to be treated for the occasion as newborn babes or heathens.

Carloman was a sturdy, independent sort of child, and when the King beckoned him he went forward to the font eagerly. He had always been able to look after himself, always been ready to laugh or to hit out in his own defense.

"If the water's cold," remarked Bertha in a whisper, "he'll dash it away."

Rhotrud shivered. "Oh, that would be an ill omen!"

They bent their heads together, the three eldest children of the King—for Gobbo had remained at home, prostrate after the journey south. The three whispered together, forgetting their surroundings, forgetting that they were in the presence of the two greatest men in Christendom. Secure in a dark corner to which they had moved in a defensive way, they were less a great King's children than a brother and two sisters leagued against a grown-up world.

Suddenly they were aware of a quick sharp mutter that had run over the company assembled in the candlelit chapel.

"Listen!" Carl said. "Listen!"

The Pope's hands were on Carloman's head.

"I baptize thee *Pepin*. In the name of the Father, and of the Son, and of the Holy Ghost. May you long hold your name in humility to God and pride of Kingship, in memory of your great grandfather Pepin, who brought to his peoples the light of the Christian world. . . ."

Carl had caught Bertha hard by the wrist and she had answered by putting her other hand as tightly on his. *Pepin?* But Gobbo was Pepin. . . .

This, then, was what the King had meant when he told Carl on the cold mountaintop that he would be his father's heir. The plan had already been made and now it had been put into practice. Sixteen years ago the King had given his eldest son the revered name of Pepin; today he had taken it away. Pepin the Hunchback, poor Gobbo, was now dispossessed not only of his inheritance but even of his name. From now on, Carloman was to be Pepin in his place.

The tension within the chapel was extreme. None there but knew the King had taken a weighty and momentous decision which might or might not lead to good. That he saw it as vital to the future they all knew too. This King they all so loved and lauded had shown them today the ruthless side of his nature. They shivered a little to realize what he sometimes allowed them to forget—that there was a man of iron hidden beneath the appearance of indulgent husband, kind father, wise and noble leader, humble scholar.

After that first sharp flick of glance to glance, the little involuntary hiss of surprise, possibly of consternation, absolute silence held the chapel.

Now the acolytes and the deacons had lit more candles. The Pope, leading in one hand Lewis and in the other the new Pepin, turned from the side chapel and began to move toward the High Altar. The King held out his hand to Hildegarde. For a second she seemed to hesitate. She looked desperately into the face of the King, as though seeking some reassurance for events that seemed to terrify her. Then she took his hand and moved stiffly at his side. Anghilbert gave Carl a quick nudge and a nod, and he too went to take his place in the procession, walking alone, with Bertha and Rhotrud behind him. There was the swish of cloth, the patter of soft shoe leather on marble as the rest of the gathering moved out from the chapel and followed the Pope toward the altar steps.

Within the sanctuary were two cushioned stools, and on these the Pope seated Lewis and Pepin. Behind them on the altar, Carl saw to his astonishment two small crowns. As the Pope knelt and began to pray, the assisting clergy were already moving forward carrying sacred oils. . . .

"I anoint thee, Pepin, King of Italy. . . . I anoint thee, Lewis, King of Aquitaine. . . ."

Carl's mind seethed and whirled with the shock and magic of the words. He stared toward the altar and saw his two little brothers sitting solemnly as they had been bidden, the crowns upon their heads. He looked again to the altar itself, as though he would see a third crown, his own, waiting to be bestowed. Then he realized that his crown rested on his father's head, that it could come to him only when his father died, for he was the heir. Confusion filled his heart as well as his intelligence. He looked frantically at his father. The King stood rigidly, immensely tall and withdrawn, his face above his golden beard as pale as wax, his eyes glittering.

"Then we shall all be kings but Gobbo," Carl thought in momentary terror. "All three of us. . . ."

There was a quick soft rustling and he saw his mother move suddenly forward. Both her arms were held out as though she would snatch the two children back from where they sat crowned and solemn. Someone's hand plucked at Hildegarde's robe. The King himself moved toward her swiftly. She looked at him wildly and faltered. Then she sank down gently into a faint so deep she seemed almost to be a dead woman lying across the altar steps.

One of the children's nurses, Adela, came from Hildegarde's room to where Carl and Bertha were staring moodily out across the courtyard.

"Is she well again?" Bertha cried, running to Adela and clasping her about the waist.

"Yes, yes—she is well enough, poor thing. Well enough."

"I thought she was dead!" Bertha said in a shaking voice. She began to cry bitterly, pressing her face into Adela's shoulder.

"Oh there, my sweet child, no more tears! Your mother sheds tears enough for all of us. Oh hush, Lady Bertha—hush now, do!"

"But what is to happen, Adela?" Carl said. "What will become of us all now? Shall we never see Lewis and Carlo—and *Pepin* again?"

"Most certainly you'll see them again!" Adela sat down on a bench against the wall and drew the pair of them to sit beside her. She put an arm round each, for she had cared for them all since they were born, she was like a second mother to them.

"The King says they are to go each to his own kingdom," Carl objected. "They are such little boys. What will become of them?"

"Why, they will be cared for and cosseted and made much of. And they will grow into splendid men—"

"But we shall not see them grow," Carl said in a low voice. "They will not be like our brothers any more, but like strangers—strange kings whose faces we hardly know."

It was even more than this that troubled him. He had long known that men called his father ruthless in necessity. He himself had never before experienced that side of the King's nature. He had lived until now as a child in the family, attending school and doing his best; aware of possible future greatness but feeling it so far away it was no more than a dream. Now he saw that he, too, was a part of the pattern his father had drawn, of which this crowning of the youngest sons was a first necessity. If this could happen, if the King for the sake of a future yet unknown could sacrifice his own young children and bring bitter sorrow to the wife he dearly loved, what more might lie in store? What fate had been decided for Carl, now openly and officially declared his father's heir? Would he, too, be sent away to grow up alone among strangers, torn from his parents and his sisters and all the friends he had made in his brief years? It was a terrible thought for the boy. At least it was possible to argue that Pepin and Lewis were too young to realize what was happening. But Carl was old enough to understand too well.

Bertha was still crying quietly, almost sleepily, with her head against Adela's plump, comfortable shoulder, when Rhotrud came to join them. She looked very pale and in some way older than when Carl had seen her only a few hours ago. Sometimes Rhotrud annoyed Carl, with her stern ways and her competent manner. But at this moment she was his sister who was as distressed as he, and he went up to her at once and put his arms round her, as he used to do when he was much younger.

"There are still the three of us," he said.

"For the time being," she agreed.

"Why—what is he going to do to me?" the boy cried in terror. "Am I to be sent away?"

Rhotrud shook her head. "Oh no, Carl! You are to be his heir, to stay with him always."

"Has he said so? I know I am to be King after him, and that Gobbo . . ." He faltered into silence. And silence held them all then. They thought, without looking at one another, of poor wayward Gobbo, who could be so spiteful or so sweet. "Rhotrud, has he said I shall stay with him always?"

"Everyone knows it, Carl. And he has spoken with Gobbo—oh, for a long, long time. He has told him how he will always be loved in his own home and family and be safe there. But he must never look for power since he is sickly."

"The King has all the wisdom of the world," Adela said softly. "He knows what is right and best. We must bend to his good will and be thankful."

"Gobbo will not be thankful," Carl replied.

"Perhaps Gobbo too," Rhotrud said. "He has always been best of all of us at school. He need not be concerned with tiresome affairs any more, that weary him and make his head ache."

Bertha roused herself. She kissed Adela, and then sat with her elbows on her knees and her chin on her fists—like a lad from the stables, Adela said.

"At least you and I cannot be sent away to be kings," Bertha said to her sister.

"Ah," cried Adela, in the knowing way that so often

made them laugh at her, "But the Lady Rhotrud has a suitor for her hand this very day. She will leave us in her turn—to be an Emperor's wife!"

"An Emperor?" cried Carl. "What Emperor?"

"The young Emperor Constantine, to be sure—the son of the Empress Irene. Envoys were here yesterday and the King has spoken with them. It is agreed, they say."

"They say also that his mother is a monster," Rhotrud said in a flat, calm voice. "And I must learn to speak Greek."

Suddenly the idea of Rhotrud as an Emperor's wife roused Carl and Bertha from their gloom. They began to laugh.

"In Byzantium where the Empress Irene rules they eat young children cooked in pies!" Carl declared.

"The women paint their hair with gold," said Bertha. "Anghilbert told me so. And they wear jewels in their noses as well as in their ears, and none must speak in the presence of any man."

"That will be dreadful for Rhotrud," Carl cried, exploding into laughter that was the noisier and sillier because he had been frightened and depressed for the past several hours. "Poor Rhotrud—they'll never silence her—she'll forever be in trouble with her tongue!"

"Hush now, for pity's sake!" Adela urged them. "You'll wake your lady mother and she is far better sleeping in her sorrow."

"What ignorant children you are," said Rhotrud

with dignity. "If I am never to speak—why must I learn Greek?"

There was no reply to that. More sober now, Carl and Bertha began to question her. But she had little to tell. Only that the offer for her hand had been made; that if their father allowed the betrothal a Greek scholar would come from Constantinople to the court of King Charles to instruct her in the tongue and the customs of the country which would one day be her own.

The King himself came then into the room where the three children were sitting with Adela.

"Go to the Queen, Adela. She is awake and asking for you."

The King wore still that distant icy look which had so startled Carl earlier. At this moment he was a desperately unhappy man. He who ruled men with confidence, with justice, with sternness where it was needed, was now thrown into utter confusion of mind by his wife's anguish. She had begged him to alter his decision, she had gone on her knees, she had wept and sobbed herself into a frenzy. She had threatened even to kill herself, or to leave him forever and return to her own home. He had destroyed his family, she said. . . .

The King now called Carl and the two girls close to him.

"Let us sit here together quietly," he said. "I shall tell you why I have done this thing, and why what I have done will be for the good of all of us in the end. One day there shall be peace and faith in all our lands because of this sacrifice. My sons will rule from the thrones I have given them, wisely and well as Christian kings. Then the world will know that because I was strong with those I most dearly loved, I set a mighty seal upon the good life. This you may not understand today. But tomorrow or the next day or the day after—you will understand and know that the King must sacrifice for his people as willingly as Abraham prepared to sacrifice to his God." He paused and, sitting there between them, he suddenly covered his eyes with his hand. "It is not easy!" he cried. "Oh dear Christ in Heaven, it is not easy!" He rose to leave them. At the door he said quietly: "Pray for me."

A few days later they left for home. They had already said good-by to four-year-old Pepin. Farther north, before they touched the Alps, Lewis the baby struck off with his retinue to the west where lay his kingdom of Aquitaine. Among those wise men who went to care for him and protect him was Anghilbert.

Bertha had said nothing when she learned that Anghilbert was to go with Lewis and supervise his education, while Arnold was to be his chief guardian. Perhaps she felt that there had been enough weeping over the past days and she must not add another tear. Or perhaps what their father had told them had stiffened and fortified her, young as she was, and so she was able to part silently with a dearly loved friend.

On that homeward journey Carl and Bertha kept

together. There was a new feeling between them, a determination that they would stay together whatever happened, that if they lost everyone else they loved somehow the two of them would contrive not to be separated. It was like a vow between them that did not need to be proposed because each knew with absolute clarity what the other thought and felt. Like Rhotrud, Carl and Bertha had grown up a great deal since they left home; when they reached the palace at Aachen once more it would be no longer as thoughtless children. The stern matters of life had come to them early and whether they liked it or not they were obliged to accept these matters and deal with them as best they could.

Hildegarde made the journey home in a litter. She barely spoke to the King, keeping her women about her, and Rhotrud, who seemed her great comfort. At the head of the column the King himself rode as proudly as ever. He had Gobbo at his side. He seemed to be making much of the boy, as though to compensate for what had gone before.

Back among the counts and the soldiers you could hear if you listened a certain soft whispering among those who remembered Gobbo's mother, the King's first wife; their allegiance was now to her son.

"Dispossessed," ran the whisper. "Disinherited . . ."

There were not many to speak the words. But enough for some others to look at one another uneasily, realizing that the King had made of his eldest son a potential enemy to whom in any discontent followers might quickly rally.

IV

The Iron King

THE KING WAS at Compline when the news
came.

It was autumn and he had gone to the chapel
wrapped in his long blue fur-lined cloak. In the quiet
and the dimness he prayed as well as he could, but
his mind was distracted by many things. In the two

44

years since the visit to Rome he had pressed forward
further and further into new realms. New conquests
had made his name more fearful and more glorious.
The pattern of the future was taking shape before
his eyes. What had once seemed an impossible dream
showed more and more promise of fulfillment. He
was subduing the pagan races in Europe one by one.
He knew well enough that baptism was sometimes
forced at the swords' points on those he had beaten
in battle. He knew that his good friend, Alcuin of
England, who now controlled the palace school, fret-
ted and frowned over this. But he knew, too, the par-
able of the sower who went forth to sow his seed.
Much of King Charles's sowing might wither or be
devoured, but some must bear fruit; and in a gen-
eration or two that in itself would have seeded a
hundredfold.

But it was of the defiant Saxons he thought as he
knelt in chapel; of Witikind, their leader, who laughed
at the efforts of Charles of the Franks to subdue this
brave and pagan people; and of the expedition that
even now had gone against the Saxons, led by the bravest warriors the King could spare from his side. . . .

"Who is to tell the King this news?"

The messenger, revived with food and wine after
his long and desperate journey, looked round him
anxiously at the grave faces of those who had listened to his tidings.

"Must I do so, my lord?" he asked Duke Eric.
"Surely he will slay me for the words I have to speak
to him!"

Young Carl was standing half hidden where the wall curved to a window slit. With him was Roriko, the Count of Maine's young son, who had been sent as a page to the King's court. The two boys kept silent, afraid that if the men realized they were there they might be sent away. With their eyes wide in their heads, and with a feeling of sick trembling, they had listened to the tale of treachery and slaughter. They dared not look at one another, for both were afraid and wished to hide the fact.

"The King will come to this chamber from the chapel," Duke Eric said to the messenger. "We will all remain with you and support you, my friend."

The counts of the palace murmured together. Over the whole gathering of them hung a cloud of grief for what had passed, fear for what might be to come. In their anxiety, in their turning one to the other in dreadful speculation, none heard the King approach. Suddenly he was there with them, standing looking toward them in surprise and interrogation.

Then indeed they turned to him at once and from their faces alone he knew that something dire had happened. As they fell back to either side of the messenger, the man moved forward and dropped on his knees.

"Lord King—I am sent with word of your army beyond the river Weser. . . ."

"What word do you bring?"

The King spoke quietly. His voice, light for a man of his build, seemed indeed little more than a whisper, as though it had died in his throat for fear of what was coming.

"Sire, my lord, King Charles . . ." the messenger faltered. "There is no army now. They are ambushed and slaughtered. The Saxon lured them on. Then with mighty force the enemy fell upon soldiers from the heights of the Suntal . . ."

"From the heights?"

"From the ridge of the mountains, my lord."

The King closed his eyes and clenched his teeth and his hands. When the enemy struck thus he struck most surely at the King's pride. It was still not so many years since the day he had sent his forces along the defile at Roncesvalles, young Roland at their head, to strike at the Moors in Spain. . . . On that day, too, the enemy struck treacherously from the mountain heights. None spoke before the King of Roncesvalles and Roland, but all remembered now.

"Well?" said the King to the messenger, between his clenched teeth. "Tell me your tale."

"They were ahead, my lord Charles," said the messenger, "and riding proudly. Geilon the Constable, Adalgis the Chamberlain, Worad the Count. They were the advance action and to support them there was Count Thierry with his army drawn up on the banks of the Rhine. My lord, Geilon and the rest were eager to fight your fight. They heard the horns blown. Thierry's men must be approaching. It was a still day and the sound echoed and seemed near. Geilon and Adalgis and the rest let out their war cry, thinking Thierry hard upon their heels. They charged to the mountain. But the Saxons were in hiding there. It was their horn which had drawn our Frankish warriors . . . Lord King, they were too few, the Saxons fresh and fierce and like a wave of armor. They fell upon our men. There was terrible slaughter. It was each man for himself and few were left to tell the tale."

The room was held in a tense and terrible silence. All eyes were upon the King standing motionless, watching the messenger as he poured out his tale.

"And then?" the King said at last.

"And then, my lord, too late there came up Count Thierry with his army. And he gathered up such fugitives as he might and rallied them and charged again. Then he, too, was slain, and the rest fled."

"The rest fled. . . ."

"Count Odilo escaped. He it was who took such command as he might. I am the count's man and am sent by him to bring this news. And to say that he is in hiding by the forests of Verden and awaits the King's command. If you will it, the count will avenge his honor and run upon his sword."

"Say to your master when you meet: 'Count Odilo, you are a Christian warrior, not a pagan Roman general.'" The King turned sharply, his long blue cloak flared out behind him as he paced the chamber. "I thank God that Count Odilo lives—that I may learn from him the names of those base brutes who so ordered the rout of my bravest men. And if God strike not, then I will strike for Him. And

I shall not leave alive one Saxon who ordered this day's work!"

At the far end of the narrow room the counts watched their King's furious pacing from wall to wall, as though in a cage he would burst open by the sheer terrible concentration of his rage and sorrow. No man dared speak any comfort. They waited, knowing that at any moment the King would decide his action and that he would expect each and every one of them to obey and follow without question wherever he might lead or direct.

Something of the King's anguish and of his fury stirred in Carl's young breast. He knew his father's ambitions, he had been quietly and privately schooled in them and vowed to silence. This confidence had made a bond between the boy and the man that was more than that of father and son. The King was to Carl his dearest father, certainly. But he was also his master, his King, his general, his model in all things. And because of this the boy had entered into the man's way of thought. He knew that Charles the King had never forgotten or forgiven the Roncesvalles disaster. He had blamed his own faulty generalship, and now, it could be seen, he was blaming himself again. There was something in the present disaster too similar to the first to be tamely endured. This was more than a defeat in the field of a mighty commander. It was a blow to the King's heart and to his pride— almost to his Faith, since the defeat had once again been effected by a heathen enemy.

There was no sound in that place but the pad and

prowl of the King's feet on the stone floor, the swish of his cloak each time he turned, the faint chink of the chain that clasped and fastened the cloak across his throat. Soon he would stop his pacing. He would speak. And on his words would depend the life and death of many men.

For perhaps the tenth time, the King came to the place where Carl and Roriko were standing. He checked abruptly.

"Carl!"

"Yes, Father?"

"You have heard this story?"

"Yes, my lord. Yes, indeed I have heard."

"Then you have heard a man's affairs and must enter into a man's life. We ride within the hour. You shall ride with us."

Carl's heart leaped like a fish at the end of a line, and as the fish must feel the bitter hook, so Carl felt the pain of extreme terror and extreme pride. He heard Roriko gasp. In envy? In fear? Carl was not certain until the moment when, speechless, he seized his father's hand and dropped on his knee as he had so often seen others do to express their complete allegiance.

Then suddenly Roriko was there beside him, only he improved the occasion by going down on both knees in his excitement.

"Lord King—take me too! Let me ride with Carl as his squire!"

There could have been no one in that gathering who expected to hear the King laugh that day. Yet at the sight of the two boys there before him Charles did indeed fling back his head and laugh loud and joyfully.

"God send me only one or two such warriors! Yes, Roriko—come with us. And if the Saxon never feared the Franks and their King before—they shall fear when they see the paladins who ride against them now!"

At the last it was hard to leave home. Rhotrud had been furiously angry when she heard that Roriko was to be one of the expedition; he was her special playfellow, he had joined her Greek lessons and worked on the books with her between lessons, so that what had seemed tedious at first had become a pleasure to her. Bertha wept because she hated to be parted from Carl, and because their mother had been ailing lately and would live in fear until he returned.

"I wish I might cut off my hair and my skirts," poor Bertha cried, "and ride with you instead of Roriko. What if you are wounded? Who will stop the blood?"

Carl scoffed and strutted, but he was careful and tender of his mother. Indeed she did look pale and worn as she bade him good-by. And although she would never hinder any boy on his way to manhood, and knew all about battles and so on, this time she held him in her arms a long time, and kissed him again and again. This he suffered patiently and kissed her in return. Then he heard the men calling him from the courtyard below the Queen's chamber. He gave Hildegarde one more hurried embrace and fled from all that he had known into the strange world of men. He passed Gobbo on the curve of the stairway.

"Oh, bold warrior!" mocked Gobbo. "Bring me back a bone or two of the enemies you carve in pieces— let's have proof of your valor!"

That had been days ago. Since then they had ridden hard. It was autumn and there was little feed for the horses. The peasants had to yield up their own winter store to the King and his army. Sometimes it was necessary to strip a barn of all it held. The wretched men and women groveled and implored. Were they and their children to starve in the bitter winter?

"All wrongs shall be redressed!" the King declared.

And the peasants were quiet because they wanted to believe this could be so, though in their hearts they must have known they would be forced to beg charity of their neighbors. They stood bareheaded, none the less, to watch the King ride by. The pale sunshine showed them his thin proud face, his bright hair and splendid beard that the breeze fanned across his breast.

"God keep him!" they said. "And his son beside him!"

His son, in fact, was bitterly distressed.

"What will they do, Father? What will they do for bread?"

"War is paid for with famine," the King replied grimly.

Possessed by his desire for vengeance, the King

swept on through the chill countryside until the great
river lay before him. Then he began scouring among
the villages and forests, rounding up small knots of
Saxons who had fled from their homes at the sound
of his approaching armor, driving them along the
river shore, ringing the forest into which they fled,
sweeping them before him like dead leaves until he
had them centering on the small settlement of Verden, which was surrounded by tall pines on three
sides and on the fourth by the swift broad river.
Here Count Odilo was in hiding and at once came
with his few surviving followers to join them.

"What will the King do now?" Roriko asked Carl
that night. Camp had been made, and they were secure in shelter, exhausted by the hard journey, though
not caring to admit as much. They lay sprawling
thankfully on a pile of skins by a glowing brazier.
"Will there be a battle?" Roriko wondered.

"How can there be a battle? They have fled before
us. No—there will be a judgment. The King will hold
a court and make trial of those who conspired and
slew Adalgis and the rest. They will be punished."

How simple it sounded—and how just. . . .

On the day after the King pitched his camp and
the Saxons were surrounded, he held his court and
had the leaders brought before him. Not Witikind,
but his lieutenants; Witikind himself had once again
eluded the net.

"I have sworn on the Cross," said Charles the King,
"that all traitors among you shall die. Deliver me those
men who plotted the Suntal ambush."

The Saxon leaders did not look at one another. They stood there before the King, five of them in a row, sturdy, flaxen-haired men with defiant blue eyes.

"Lord King," said their spokesman at last, "give us leave to consider this together."

"What consideration is necessary? It is plain what you must do. Name and deliver the traitors and when I see that you are without guile I will thereafter use clemency."

"There are many who conspired," said another Saxon. "We must name all—but none who are in fact innocent. Give us then leave, as our leader demands, to speak privately, that no mistake be made."

"I will agree to this," the King said at last. "I admit the necessity. Return in two hours."

The Saxons went away and the King and his camp set about their midday meal. The King ate heartily, with Carl at his right hand and Duke Eric at his left. Roriko was with the stewards and the squires. Sometimes Carl looked across at him. It seemed to him that Roriko was eating sparingly. And indeed Carl, too, was picking at his food, which was by no means usual. But in his stomach, as well as in his mind, there was a feeling of unease and queasy anticipation.

In the early afternoon the King sat again in his court. It was a crisp and sunny day and the court was held in a clearing in the center of the village. The King sat on a great wooden stool that had been dragged out from a nearby dwelling in the manor. Round him stood his counts and advisers.

"They are behind their time," said Duke Eric. "It would have been wiser to take hostages."

But as he spoke there was a stirring and a movement beyond the edge of the clearing. The Saxons were returning. First came those leaders who had come to the court that morning. Behind them could be seen others, moving forward slowly but without faltering.

The leaders came to within a few yards of the King.

"These are the traitors," said their spokesman. "We have them here, every man of them, confessed and ready to accept their punishment."

Over the heads of the leaders the King and the rest saw drawn up in rank on rank every Saxon who had fallen into the Frankish net, every warrior, every fugitive who had been driven to this place and encircled. Silently they stood and gazed toward the King, awaiting his next word.

The King looked over the ranks. It was impossible to count how many had come there. The clearing was full and beyond the clearing could be seen the heads of short men and tall, lean and stolid, young and old, waiting in silence for the King to pass judgment upon them.

"How many traitors?"

"Four thousand, Lord King, and five hundred more."

Then he looked up at Charles for the first time. His gaze was calm and triumphant. Unarmed and surrounded as he and his men were, he still felt himself the victor. It had needed great courage to play this particular hand.

The King returned the Saxon's gaze. He stood there as a king of steel and stone might stand, in whom only the eyes seem living. The rest of him was held rigid in the grip of a fearful necessity and the terror of it blazed in his eyes like frost on iron. This was the moment on which depended the entire future. To be weak now was to destroy all he had striven for, all he had so far achieved.

Silence hung like a great burden over all that gathering. There was no movement, no sign or sound of life save a bird singing in a bare tree and the rushing of the river near at hand.

Then at last the King spoke. His voice was quiet, yet every word rang on the air and echoed in the further silence.

"I have sworn," he said. "This was my vow before Almighty God, his Blessed Saints, my own honor and the honor of my dead. Where there was no guile there could have been clemency, as also I promised. But is not this guile? Speak—if you dare deny it!" Still the silence held. Then the King spoke once more. "Death is my answer. No Saxon of you leaves this place alive."

No one moved. But over the great concourse of men standing in the last of the autumn sunlight there ran a strange and terrible groan, as though their grief could not be contained by their courage but must burst out once in anguish.

"So be it," replied the Saxon leader at last. "If this is the sacrifice your God requires—let it be made. Only we ask that you remember us, each and every one.

Also the widows and the orphans you will make this day, whose curses we shall be powerless to deny."

"Silence!" The King turned on his heel. He brushed by Duke Eric as he went but he did not raise his eyes. "See to it," he said. Then he strode away to his tent and was hidden from view.

Among the press of the men he now knew so well, Carl felt Roriko groping for his hand. He clasped it and began to shoulder his way out of the crowd, dragging the younger boy with him. Once free, they began to run. They ran hard over the cold ground and into the deep black shadows of the pine forest. Carl knew he must keep his head or they would lose themselves; he marked the way as he had been taught to from his youngest days, noting a tree stump here, a broken branch there, fungus on a mound, a sharp green fern growing where water trickled over lichened boulders. . . . At last they came to a place where a tree or two had been felled. The biggest branches had been hauled to one side and chopped in lengths, the ground was covered with the fresh-smelling chips that had flown from the blade of the ax. The small branches, still bearing their dark green needles and russet cones, were heaped up against a mound. The two boys, breathless and spent by now, threw themselves on the heap and lay there side by side, trying to get back their breath, trying not to see with the quick eyes of imagination the picture of cold slaughter that even now was being painted in blood at the river's bank.

Roriko was sobbing. He was a year younger than Carl and Carl was not so very old himself. He knew that if he comforted Roriko with soft words he would catch the infection of tears and collapse in his turn.

"He had to do it!" he shouted suddenly in that quiet place. "He had to do it, Roriko! What would have happened, else? They would have laughed in his face! They dared him and he had to be strong! He had to be! He had to be!"

And in his terrible distress, Carl fell on Roriko and started pummeling him, so that they rolled fighting and striking out at one another furiously, down from the heap of boughs to the floor of the clearing with its slippery matting of pine needles and splinters of wood.

Carl had bloodied Roriko's nose and Roriko had blacked Carl's eye before they came to their senses. Then they helped one another, staggering, to the heap of branches and sank down there, utterly exhausted. Roriko fell straight into a heavy sleep. But Carl stayed a long time with his knees bunched tight against his chin, and now it was he who wept most bitterly. He sat there struggling to understand, to accept what he himself had tried to impress upon Roriko—that the King had been forced to brutality, that otherwise all would have been lost, all thrown away that he had achieved till now. Yet what he might have thrown away by this deed itself did not bear contemplation. When he thought he had come to an understanding of his father, Carl's tears still flowed. He was too weary to

stop them. Or perhaps they were tears for his childhood which lay finally in ruins behind him. He could
never be a carefree boy again.

When the next day came, men hardly spoke at all.
They struck camp and rode away thankfully, though
without any joy in their hearts, from a place that
had become accursed. In their great grave the Saxon
warriors lay, and the King shut his mind to pity, while
his followers tried vainly to rid their thoughts of yesterday's horrors.

The journey home seemed to stretch ahead of
them like a pilgrimage, utterly stony and comfortless.
At the next camp the King took counsel with Duke
Eric and the counts. He was loath to leave this country unpoliced. He began to lay plans for dividing his
force, leaving half to keep peace in this wild and defiant region; the rest would return to winter at home.

"I myself shall leave you," the King said. "My son
shall remain in my place."

Carl looked helplessly at his father but could get
no answering glance of reassurance. He was glad that
Duke Eric, standing close behind, put a hand on his
shoulder in a warm, comfortable grasp.

His father had not spoken to Carl of the Saxon
massacre. Perhaps he felt that between the two of
them no explanation was required, and in a way this
was true. In his father's silence Carl rightly recognized acknowledgment of his own good sense that
could accept, even without understanding, the dilemma

of a great Christian King. He for his part tried by quiet devotion, by attending to his father's small needs before they were expressed, to make plain his undiminished trust and affection. The partnership between them grew up in these few days like a great tree touched by magic.

Therefore it was a double blow to the boy to learn that he must now be parted from the King as well as from the home and family he was missing bitterly already.

It was on the fourth day, the day before the armies would divide and go their ways, that they were met by a messenger carrying letters from home. They had made their camp and were preparing food when the man arrived, directed by peasants who had seen the passing of the army. The letters were brought to the King by the messenger himself, as the custom was, that none might ever say he had failed in his duty, or pretend that the letters had gone astray.

One letter was from Alcuin and the King seized on it with joy. For the first time in all these long days, he smiled. Then gloom returned. For what would Alcuin, the uncompromising, have to say about what had taken place at Verden?

"See the messenger well fed," the King told Carl, then turned at once to his letter.

Carl went with the messenger toward the fires where the meat was roasting. The fires shone through the blue dusk and the fine tempting smell of the meat filled the air.

"How are they at home?" Carl asked eagerly. "Is

my mother well again? Does my sister Bertha send me any message?"

Before the man could reply, there was a sudden cry from the King's tent, a cry of such anguish and bitter rage that Carl spun on his heel in horror.

The messenger caught his arm hard.

"Leave him, Lord Carl. He has a great grief to bear. One of the greatest that could come to him. . . ." He looked steadily and pitifully at the shrinking boy. "He has lost his dearly loved wife."

For a second Carl did not take in what had been said.

"His dearly loved wife . . ."

"The Queen—our beautiful Lady Hildegarde . . . Your mother."

"Lost?" Carl's voice was lost too. He could hardly whisper the next dreadful question. "Do you mean she is dead?"

"She died four days ago. May the good Lord rest her sweet soul. God give you strength, poor lad—and the King too—to bear it."

Four days ago the Saxons had come to the King's court, the sentence had been passed and carried out. . . .

Carl put his hands on the messengers arms and gave them a warm, steady pressure. Then he turned and went quickly to his father's tent.

V

Fastrada

WHEN CARL RETURNED to his home many
months later he had become a soldier. True,
he had seen no mighty battles; but he had been en-
gaged in many small skirmishes, and even the least
conflict with an opposing force must turn a boy fast

and painfully into a soldier. Roriko, too, had changed. He had grown tall and hard, almost as tall as Carl in spite of the one-year difference in their ages. Roriko longed for the day when he would grow a beard and was forever hopefully fingering his chin. For Carl, this outward symbol of manhood seemed less important than the increasing steadiness of his own intentions. He was consciously modeling himself on his father now, not only in purpose but by copying his walk, his gestures, his voice. Once he had heard Count Odilo call him "our fledgling King." And sometimes Roriko called him Carling, which in a punning fashion meant Young King.

They rode together now, Carl and Roriko, as they approached Aachen, where the King was settled for the winter. Though he and the family had always been on the move, shifting from palace to palace as the needs of state demanded, Aachen had always seemed most like home to all of them.

"Will Rhotrud be watching from the walls, do you suppose?" Carl asked—and laughed slyly as Roriko turned a slow and unlovely scarlet. "What if she's found a playmate she likes better? Absence is dangerous to affection, so Count Odilo says."

"The Lady Rhotrud will please herself, of course," Roriko replied almost primly.

"Oh, I shall be glad to see my sisters again!" Carl cried in sudden excitement, forgetting to tease Roriko, forgetting his own dignity.

"And your father, the King, too, Carl. I wish I might be going to see my father. He will have forgotten me by now, and my mother will, too. It is three whole years since I left home."

At the mention of Roriko's mother, Carl flinched. His father and his sisters and his eldest brother he might find, but not his mother any more.

"I wonder if Gobbo is at Aachen," he said, to divert both his thoughts and Roriko's. "And has he still thoughts of becoming a monk? The King would make him an Abbot, I daresay. He has made my aunt Gisela Abbess of Chelles."

He went on talking, gossiping about the family, remembering a wealth of detail he had half forgotten and now scratched up out of his memory in his eagerness to feel nearer to them all. There was a hope of spring in the air today and the sun shone as they came near the end of their journey.

Then, as they came towards the city, a clarion call sounded from the King's palace. At once the horns of the returning column answered. The air was filled with clamor. Men shouted with pleasure of the homecoming, and cheers and cries greeted the sight of a small band of horse that came clattering out of the palace yard and galloped at full stretch to meet them.

The horsemen—there were about twenty—were led by two figures, in streaming, colored cloaks and feathered caps, mounted on a line chestnut and a roan whose bright caparisons shone and glittered in the sunlight.

Carl suddenly let out a great shout and spurred forward, yelling to Roriko to follow. "It's Bertha! It's Rhotrud!" he cried.

They pounded across the intervening space, fanned out and passed the laughing girls, wheeled sharply and reined in to ride on either side of them. Then in an instant all four were dismounted. Carl seized Bertha and was hugging her until she shrieked; while Rhotrud and Roriko, only a shade more formal, caught each other hard by the hands and stood there laughing and breathless, overcome by their pleased confusion at seeing one another again.

"We're home!" Carl cried. He pushed Bertha aside and seized Rhotrud round the waist. "Sisters, you've become fine ladies! What do you think of us?"

"Not that you're fine gentlemen!" Bertha retorted. "Oh Rhotrud—look how soldierly they are! Why, the great coarse creatures! And I thought they might still be dear, nice little boys!"

"I'm glad they're not," said Rhotrud. And she gave Roriko a bold, sweet smile, so that he began once more to blush his own particularly violent shade of red.

Now the rest of the two parties had come up with the King's children. There were loud and eager greetings. Those who were home-coming complimented the princesses; those who had remained at home praised the King's son and heir, so greatly grown, and the handsome young squire who attended him. Everyone talked at once. Men inquired for their wives and families; sometimes the news was good and made them laugh with pleasure, sometimes less excellent so that they looked anxious and grew impatient to be away to see for themselves which child was ailing, or why a brother's widow was behind with paying her taxes, or where the family was lodged since the house burned down a month ago.

Rhotrud and Bertha, Carl and Roriko remounted and Carl turned toward the city. Rhotrud reached out and laid a hand on his bridle.

"Wait. Let the others go. There is something you must know. It is about our father."

At that Roriko, tactful and courteous, waved a quick farewell and rode off to join the column. Rhotrud, Carl and Bertha were left together as the rest rode away toward the palace.

"He is not ill?" Carl cried.

"No—he is well enough. His health is excellent."

"There is some other trouble then—something that distresses him?"

"Nor is he distressed," said Bertha.

The two girls looked at one another uneasily.

"Carl—" Rhotrud's voice was at once gentle and severe, echoing those earlier days when she had tried to rule the other children—"we all know how he loved our mother. Oh it was dreadful to see him, his terrible grief when he came riding home and she was already buried. Those were fearful days."

"He will never forget her, Carl," Bertha put in. "You know that as well as we do."

It seemed to Carl that they were defending their father against some charge that was not even made. They looked at one another and then at him, they were anxious and very ill at ease.

"What is it you want to tell me?" he cried at last.

But in his heart he suddenly knew and shrank from having his fears confirmed. Yet how unreasonable those fears were. "Tell me," he said more gently.

"If you will try to understand . . ."

"I will try."

Rhotrud spoke the words he knew he must hear.

"He has taken another wife, Carl. He married some months ago. We have a stepmother now. . . ."

Gobbo was standing halfway up the flight of steps to the King's apartments. He heard Carl coming and turned. He stood with his hands on his hips, waiting for Carl to reach his side. This was his favorite posture now; back to the wall, that the hump might be hidden, two or three steps above the next man to give him some height. He was handsomer than ever but his expression had darkened as it was bound to do by nature of his sad circumstances. He was smiling, not with pleasure at seeing his brother again, but in a mocking way Carl thought offensive. Had someone suggested once that Gobbo yearned after the monastic life? Carl found it hard to believe.

"I know where you are bound, Carl. To greet the Queen."

"To greet the King," Carl replied. "And his new wife. How are you faring, Gobbo?"

"Neither so far nor so fast as you, brother," Gobbo replied.

Carl saw no need to reply to that. He smiled briefly, clapped Gobbo on the arm in passing, and went his way to his father.

He found the King with his new clerk, Einhard, busy about letters to Pope Hadrian and to young Pepin of Italy, the brother Carl could now barely remember.

As Carl entered, the King thrust aside the papers that had been spread before him. He rose, and holding out his arms seized Carl in a huge embrace.

"God bless you, my son! I hear great accounts of your generalship."

"I am the humblest soldier of all, Father—an apprentice to generals, no more!"

"Well, you have earned a high opinion. . . . It is good to see you at home again, boy. This is Einhard, who has come to be one of us here. He is the most skilled scribe you might hope to meet."

"And the King's servant, and yours, sir," young Einhard said to Carl.

He was very small—small-boned, short, slim—at court they had already nicknamed him. They called him Dwarfling, but in fondness rather than malice. His fair, honest face was full of devotion for the King.

"And I have more news for you, Carl," the King cried.

"Have they told you I am wed again?"

"Yes, Father."

"A King needs a wife, Carl—more, perhaps, than most men. Do you understand?"

Carl looked steadily at his father. "I try to understand, my lord."

It was perhaps the first time he had spoken with such formality to his father. The words themselves were nothing, they were familiar; but there was a chilly dignity in his voice that was the more telling for being so like the King's own chilly dignity when he was displeased. A look of pain passed over Charles's face, but it vanished quickly. He smiled at his son, but a little sadly.

Before he could speak again a woman, a stranger, came through the far archway toward them.

"Come here, Fastrada," the King said, "and speak to my son."

Fastrada held out her hands as she advanced. No one could have seemed friendlier. She was smiling. She was a handsome woman with fine coils of bright hair; but the smile which should have warmed her face and opened it, as it were, in welcome to Carl seemed to him only to adorn it like a mask. Her mouth smiled, but her eyes were too blue, too piercing to share the warmth, and so it quickly died away.

"Then you are Carl," she said, holding him at arm's length and appraising him. "Welcome home. Stay long in Aachen. Your sisters miss you."

As I, thought Carl, miss my mother. . . . Aloud he replied conventionally, thanking her for her welcome, wishing her happiness in her marriage. He was surprised at his own calm. He felt, in some curious way, that his meeting with Fastrada had tried his new capabilities more severely than any encounter he had had in the field.

It was strange, after so much that was new and hard to endure, to return to palace life. Carl had forgotten much. Now the palace school flourished under

Alcuin, its master these many years. What had seemed a vain ambition when King and scholar first met had been encompassed with success. Never before had the palace school shone so brightly, attracted so many wandering scholars from other lands. The studies that were founded in the school spread, too, to scholarly diversions within the court. Eagerly they disputed together, on religion and philosophy and mathematics and poetry. Each gave the other a nickname that their worldly distinctions might be lost; the King was David—Alcuin was Horace. They called Rhotrud Columba, the Dove. And quietly and wisely as a dove she walked and talked with her returned playmate Roriko. The Greek betrothal seemed to be forgotten.

At table, his new Queen beside him, the King ate hugely and in silence, while one scholar or another read aloud. Of all the books the King most loved to hear was the great work of St. Augustine, *De Civitate Deo* (*The City of God*). It was never known which of those who had the gift of good reading would be chosen to read aloud at any particular meal. Suddenly the King would point to the one he had elected reader for the day. Then the reader must leave his meat and take his place at the lectern where the book was opened—and he'd be lucky if there was anything but pickings left for him when the meal was done.

But all diversions were not scholarly at Aachen. The King had had a great bath made in the palace, of the kind the Romans knew how to build. There he loved to swim, and his followers with him, sometimes two hundred men at a time, splashing and shouting in the water.

The King, too, was a great huntsman, and the forests and the plain yielded excellent sport. They hunted wild boar for the most part; but there were wolves to be routed out too, and in the mountains there were bears. There was a heady excitement about those clear smooth days of early spring, still with a tang of frost at morning and evening. The hunt streamed from the gates of the palace at first light, the horses clattering and striking sparks from the rough cobbles, then thudding on the turf and heather of the tracks, broad and narrow, that carried them into the wild countryside.

The King rejoiced in the company of his children on these hard hunting days. The girls rode out with the rest, with half a dozen other ladies. When at noon they paused to water their horses at some river or some stream and took their food hot on skewers from the fires the laughter of the women rang through the clearings. Sometimes Gobbo rode with them for half a day, then detached himself and made for home, riding between two of his tallest squires, wearing a voluminously cut cloak that he might conceal his crooked back from prying eyes. Fastrada remained at home, for she was soon to give birth to her first child.

Fastrada . . . It was not a name that made men smile. . . .

The vigorous life at Aachen existed within a framework, rigid and inflexible, ruled by the feasts and the offices of the Church. If you woke at night and turned on your bed, you might hear the monks chanting in the chapel on the far side of the courtyard around which the palace and its various annexes were built. And if you should rise to look from the window upon the still dark night, then you might see the King himself, striding in his long blue cloak toward the chapel to pray. For he slept lightly. He rose often. Sometimes he would take up his cloak and go to the chapel. Sometimes in those small hours of half-darkness he might take from beneath his pillow the writing tablets he kept there always. Then he would practice his Greek alphabet, which always gave him trouble, writing out by way of exercise one of the prayers Alcuin had composed for him, or Bishop Fuldrada of St. Denis, or Paul the Deacon. . . .

When Carl first cried out bitterly against his father's new marriage, Alcuin had rebuked him.

"He needed distraction from his great grief," Alcuin said. "When you are older you will understand how it was with him."

In his heart Carl understood already—only his comprehension differed from Alcuin's friendly sympathy. It was not only distraction from grief at losing Hildegarde that the King had been in need of—he had desperately desired some means of diverting his thoughts from the blackness that had held them fast since the massacre at Verden.

Carl had not been home more than a few days before he discovered an uneasiness at court. As the spring wore on through its pleasant days he traced the trouble increasingly to Fastrada. The King was changed by his marriage, they said. His restless energy was held in check by the toils of his passion for his new Queen. Instead of expending that energy on brilliant statesmanship and prowess in the field, he stayed at home and eased his own temper in small despotisms that made those who loved and served him restless.

But their loyalty to him was great; they respected him as a ruler, as a warrior, as a man of God, and as a noble friend. They could not bring themselves to blame him entirely.

"It is the Queen who has bewitched him. Fastrada has him spellbound, he speaks with her tongue. And that tongue is a cruel one."

They were waiting to see him rouse up and plan fresh sorties among the savage tribes he had sworn to bring to the true faith. But when these plans were made they were made for others; the King, it seemed, would remain at home.

"He dare not leave her," someone said, "for fear she plots against him in his absence. He knows her to be false, yet his manhood is in thrall to her."

Listening to these murmurings Carl was increasingly troubled. He was puzzled, too, by the way Gobbo attached himself at this time to the brother who had displaced him.

"It is not easy to endure a stepmother," Gobbo said. "Have I not suffered myself?"

"Your stepmother was my mother, Gobbo. Do not speak of her in the same breath as you speak of Fastrada."

"Truly, she did treat me as her own. I am false if I say otherwise," Gobbo admitted; and his handsome dark face lighted suddenly into the smile he allowed himself so rarely nowadays. "No—she took me, she did not disown me. It was my father who saw fit to do that."

"He did not do it easily," Carl said.

"Easily or hardly, it makes no difference to me. You others are all to be kings, but a monastery is good enough for me."

"It is good enough for better men," Carl replied impatiently, "and the choice will be your own."

"I hope so, Carl."

"How could it be otherwise? As for Lewis and—and Pepin, I wonder what joy they have of their thrones, alone there, away from us all."

"Oh, they have forgotten us by now!" Gobbo cried. "Be sure of that. Just as Rhotrud," he added slyly, "has forgotten she is the betrothed of the Empress's son Constantine."

There had been dancing in the great hall that night, a troupe of savage fellows had been brought in by their master, who claimed to be a Christian Turk, and they had stamped and shouted and clapped their hands to the thin music of pipes. Carl looked now across the floor of the hall to where Rhotrud was sitting with Roriko of Maine. There was an air about them of contented companionship. They were young to speak of love but it seemed to Carl that they did already love one another. Perhaps for the first time Carl wondered in a vague and rather bewildered way who would be his wife. Some princess from beyond the seas perhaps, a stranger to whom he would give devotion and a home and children.

The evening was ending. The King and Fastrada rose and retired. The gathering gradually broke up and soon the great hall was empty of all but the seneschal directing the servants in clearing the boards and setting the place to rights; and the cellarer and the chief butler supervising the wine jars and drinking vessels.

Carl had not moved from his place and neither had Gobbo. Afterward he realized that it was Gobbo who had kept him there, gossiping idly. When at last Carl yawned and began to rise, Gobbo put a hand on his arm.

"Here's Count Odo and young Hugo to speak with you, Carl. And Irmin and Walatho."

Carl looked in astonishment at the men who had moved up behind him and now, hemming him in, stood waiting for his attention.

"What is the matter, my lords?" he asked.

"Lord Carl," said Count Odo, "may we speak freely?"

"How else?" Carl asked cautiously.

"We wish only to say one thing," Count Odo replied in a low, grave voice. "It is this: No good can come to the land or to the Church while the King is thus bewitched. He speaks not with his own voice, but with another's."

"We fear greatly for his many enterprises," put in Walatho. "Conquests well made must be maintained. His gains will slip through his hands."

"He dallies where he should be doing," said Irmin.

Carl frowned. "I know these things are said."

"Lord Carl," said Count Odo. "What we have to say is brief. If the lords among themselves should think right to take another King—they look to you to lead them."

In utter bewilderment Carl stared from one face to the next. All looked grave and even distressed. He felt that these were honest men who had come to a hard decision. Yet he knew their loyalty was not enough or they could not have come to him. . . . He realized with a terrible feeling of shock that he was the center of a conspiracy. He was being offered a crown. Not a crown in the far distant future, but an immediate crown taken by force from the head of his own father. . . .

It was so preposterous that before he knew what he was doing, Carl had laughed. Instantly the circle of faces hardened. The men who had placed themselves in his young hands glanced at one another sharply, then at Gobbo.

"What now?" one said.

"He will betray us!" said another sharply.

Carl realized that it was in his power to destroy them all. It was an appalling thought. He turned away and at once there was a sharp movement of a hand to a dagger. Then Gobbo moved too. His hand covered the threatening hand and he shook his head. As

Carl crossed the floor of the great hall, it was Gobbo
who came after him and caught him by the arm as
he went through the archway into the gallery beyond.

"Carl—Carl, they are my friends and yours."

"But not the King's."

"What will you do? Will you betray us?"

"If I do—he will kill them."

"Then he must kill me too, brother—for I am one
of them."

"You fool, Gobbo! Unless you swear a solemn oath
to quit these traitors," Carl cried fiercely, "I will go to
the King now, whether or not you are my brother!"

Gobbo sighed. Then he shrugged. "Very well. I shall
swear. I can answer for the others. Believe that or
not, as you wish. I have not many friends—but I
have these few. They will do as I say."

Carl hesitated. He had not the experience to deal
with this and he was bound to acknowledge the fact.
Though he would have gone to the King with the
names of the conspirators, he could not harden his
heart toward Gobbo. He knew him far better than
those other brothers who had been sent away in childhood and he had not the strength to betray him.

"They must leave the court," Carl said at last. "See
to that or I will indeed go to the King. I swear in
my turn."

"Swear too," said Gobbo, "that you will forget what
you have heard."

Carl looked steadily at Gobbo. "I shall be ashamed
to remember," he replied.

A curious expression crossed Gobbo's handsome

face—part relief, part shame, part tender affection for his half brother. He shrugged once more and turned back into the great hall.

Carl watched him go. He saw him approach the conspirators and how they drew round him. Gobbo, too, was a king's son. It had always been possible that men might see in him a center for revolt. But all Carl could think of then was how Gobbo had said, *I have not many friends. . . .* He shuddered. He would forget what he had heard and seen; he would forget because he must.

VI

Kings Meet

NOW IF I had the eye and the wings of a bird, Carl thought—rather fancifully, since he looked upon himself as a plain soldier—I should be able to see great numbers of people converging on this place.

I should see young Lewis, riding across Europe from his kingdom of Aquitaine. And Pepin, King of Italy, who must by now have crossed the Alps and be headed this way. I should see my father's vast lands, stretching from ocean to ocean, prospering in the new ways. And only the Saxon lands should I see desolate; beaten, subdued, laid waste. But there, too, I might see men riding, a whole long column of them, and in their midst a mighty chieftain and his kinsman, proud and wary, coming at last to conference with the King. . . .

He was standing on the tower parapet. A soft air blew from the plain, laden with the scent of things newly growing, of the earth freed after snow and the sudden uprush of sap stilled too long by the cold winter. He was filled with nervous anticipation of the days to come. He had not met his two brothers since the parting in Italy, he could not even remember the faces of the babies they were then. How would they greet one another? What would there be to say once the greeting was over?

But most of all Carl was nervous because he knew that so much depended on whether the Saxon chiefs arrived or stayed away. Count Amalwin had traveled on an embassy to Witikind, carrying with him an invitation to the Saxon chief to attend the King where he held his court that spring at Paderborn. Now at last, after the years of vengeance, stalemate had been reached. Two proud men had fought one another to a standstill and now a new approach had to be found. The King chose generosity. Count

Amalwin's journey was the result. He was to leave hostages with the Saxons and return with Witikind and his deputy chieftain, his kinsman Abbion. . . .

Someone came up to Carl and put an arm across his shoulders, then leaned beside him on the parapet. He did not need to turn his head to know that Bertha had joined him.

"Is there any sign yet?" she asked.

"Not yet."

"Let it be soon!" Bertha said softly. The words were almost a prayer. Carl turned, then, to look at her. It was not the arrival of the Saxon chiefs that Bertha cared about nor even of their young brother Pepin, who had once been Carloman. She watched for Lewis and his train, for with Lewis would come Anghilbert, and even after this long lapse of years Bertha stayed steadfast. Carl frowned slightly. Bertha was no longer a child but a marriageable young girl. Her youthful fondness for her tutor had turned to love and she had vowed lately in all seriousness what she had mockingly sworn in childhood—that she would marry no other man.

"It is a long time, Bertha," Carl said. He put his arm round her fondly. "What if he has a wife by now?"

"Then it will be as I have vowed. I shall marry no other."

She did not smile, but looked steadily at her brother. The wind was whipping her fair hair across her cheek. The scarlet cloak she had thrown over her shoulders lifted and billowed against the rough stone of the parapet. Suspense and her own deep sincerity had made her pale.

"And the King . . . ?" Carl said doubtfully. "If Rhotrud is to marry the Empress's son—are you to be content with a mere scholar?"

Bertha laughed then. "Oh, I will be content! And we have a father who wants us to be happy—who loves us, Carl."

Carl did not answer her. He could not bring himself to speak against the King, to remind Bertha that if personal happiness stood in the way of the future their father had planned, then personal happiness must go—as it had had to go before now. Nor did he want to take away from his sister the delight of anticipating her reunion with Anghilbert.

Somewhere hidden in Bertha was the same vein of iron determination that was in the King, their father. Their stepmother Fastrada could make no impression on Bertha. She went her own way and was unmoved by the factions and intrigues of the court. It was to Bertha alone that Carl had confided the approach of the counts in that first year of their father's remarriage. There had been no further signs of revolt. Murmurings against the Queen yes, there were still plenty of those. But none spoke now against the King. Yet perhaps there was still a watchfulness, a waiting for some moment no one named, when the King would be his absolute self again.

The King, emerged from his first infatuation, was indeed nearer his true self. He strode about his castles as he strode about his kingdom, a man mighty enough to straddle a continent. If he was a man in whom these days the iron of the warrior was more apparent than the warm heart of the leader they had so greatly loved, none regretted that openly. These days were days that demanded iron. And from the man who had ordered the massacre of Verden, what else but ruthless strength was to be looked for?

"Is that a column riding?" Carl cried suddenly. He peered out toward the horizon. "We need Gobbo's long sight."

"Where?" she cried. "Where—where? I can see nothing!"

"To the west. Between the line of the trees, moving down the incline. On the far side of the water—look!"

"Yes—oh yes, Carl! There are horses! Look quickly —now! There is a long, long column winding down the slope. From the west, Carl?"

"It is Lewis!"

But she corrected him, her face glowing. "It is Anghilbert!" she said.

When the horns sounded the King was in council. He had been sitting with Alcuin and three of the bishops, and they had talked long and earnestly about the schools that must be set up in the dominions of Charles the King. It was no longer enough that the palace school flourished under its great master, Alcuin. It should serve only for a model for more and more.

"The day must come," the King said, "when every man's son shall go to school—yes, and his daughters too."

The monasteries needed their own schools, for many of the monks were necessarily illiterate men.

"The sentiments they write to me are good," the King went on, tapping a parchment that lay before him, "but the language is uncouth—the unlettered tongue failing through ignorance. Thus men cannot with dignity and worthiness interpret their own pious devotion. Worse, they must often misinterpret the Holy Scriptures."

"We need many teachers," Alcuin agreed. "It must needs be slow, this growth of knowledge. But none the less strong for that."

"We need teachers who are still humble enough to be the pupils of wiser men," the King said. "Would that I had twelve clerks so learned in all wisdom and so perfectly trained as were Jerome and Augustine!"

Alcuin smiled. "The Maker of heaven and earth has not many such men—and do you expect to have twelve?"

"If it should seem wise to you, my lord King," one of the bishops said, "it would be well to draw up a capitulary—a letter to be sent under your seal to all monasteries and seats of learning, setting out your plan and your desires."

The rest murmured in agreement. Charles glanced at his secretary, ever devotedly at his elbow: "What do you say, Einhard? Shall you and Alcuin and I between us contrive such a document? And you shall correct me and set my language straight," he added, "for I, too, am a poor scholar—though the good Lord knows I am eager to learn."

And it was now that the ringing voice of the horn shouted its message.

The King looked up in keen anticipation. He snapped his fingers for a messenger.

"Go instantly and discover whether it is one of my sons approaching—or the Saxon chiefs."

He rose as the man leaped to the command. There was a great conflict in him, a longing for his sons, yet a keen desire to know the Saxons had responded to the new approach. He went out onto the gallery and almost at once the horns sounded again and an immense clatter and clamor filled the courtyard below.

"Alcuin!" the King shouted. "I think they are both come! My two boys are here . . . Hildegarde's sons . . ." He gripped Alcuin's arm and for a moment his half-forgotten self shone clearly in his eyes. "They will not know me, Alcuin. . . . They will not know their father. . . ."

Then Carl came up the stone stairway, taking the steps a couple at a time. He was flushed with excitement. Try as he would, he could not take this reunion calmly.

"Father, they're here! Both in the same moment! Lewis and Pepin, both! Your two young kings, my lord!"

"My *three* young kings," said his father. He put

his arm across Carl's shoulder and embraced him warmly. "What are they like?" he asked in an exaggerated whisper.

Before Carl could reply the clamor below increased. The shouting of men, the cries of greeting were now overlaid by the high sweet voices of the sisters. Carl heard them crying to the new arrivals: "Come quickly to the King! Come to your father, Lewis—Pepin! Let him see how you are grown from babies into monarchs! Quickly—quickly! He is waiting!"

Then they came surging up the stairway, the girls with a brother apiece caught by the arm, pulling and tugging them in a manner completely without dignity, pushing them at last so that they stood side by side before the King himself, smoothing their hair and their tunics that had become disordered in the flurry.

Over the tumult as men crowded in behind the two princesses to get a sight of the newcomers, a slow silence settled down as the King contemplated his sons.

There they stood, officially come to give to the King of the Franks that oath of allegiance that was made regularly by all vassal lords. One was a tall dark stripling with a merry face; the other smaller, more still, fair, pale, blue-eyed. Not much more than a child yet, this youngest son, but with an imperious flare to his nostrils that spoke of a stubborn will and a sharp temper.

The King held out his arms.

"My children!" he said. "My children!"

At that the merry-eyed Pepin stepped forward eagerly into his father's embrace, kissing him and hugging him, and crying out in loud greeting: "Oh I have dreamed of this! I have dreamed of it night after night! You gave me a kingdom, Father, but this is my home!"

Laughing delightedly, hugely, the King with his arm still about Pepin's shoulders, held out his other hand to young Lewis.

The boy stepped forward. Falling on one knee, he took the King's hand and kissed it in fealty and homage.

"God save you, my lord King," he said. "Thus speaks your vassal king, Lewis of Aquitaine."

It must have been Bertha who gave a quick nervous giggle. As she did so, Fastrada came sweeping in from her own apartments.

"Be silent!" said King Charles sharply to his daughter. He glanced at Fastrada, then back to his youngest son. "Lewis, I see, is already a man of the world. Pepin—look how your young brother outstrips you in manners."

Pepin flushed. He dropped on his knee and made him homage honestly enough, though briefly.

"And to the Queen likewise, your greeting, my sons," the King said.

Pepin, still on his knee, kissed Fastrada's extended hand courteously. Lewis, however, had already risen. He bowed slightly, briefly touched her hand, then stepped aside.

Carl watched Lewis in uneasy amazement. The

boy had turned a joyous family meeting into a state occasion. If it had not been that Anghilbert came in his train, Carl would have wished this youngest brother back in his own distant realms, where he could strut as he pleased without hindrance or applause from any of them here today.

By nightfall the Saxon chiefs had not arrived, nor did any outrider bring warning of their near approach. The King chose to be undisturbed. His attention was all for his sons and he had forgotten that half his purpose in summoning them had been to have them there as witnesses to a great triumph. He wanted them beside him, kings surrounding the King, when Witikind the Saxon, his oldest and most obdurate enemy, came face to face with him at last.

But for the moment Charles the King seemed ready to forget the deeper issues. The time was ripe for seeing how the boys were shaping. Reports from tutors and ambassadors were one thing; their actual presence to make their own accounting was a more impressive matter.

Shrugging off the slight chill that had fallen over the first greeting, the King proclaimed a feast. It was still Lent and he knew that Alcuin shook his head, however gently. The King was fond of his food; he needed his food, he always said, and fasting made him ill.

"I shall not be grudged this celebration," he assured Alcuin. "I am a father with two sons returned— though I would call neither prodigal. We shall feast, then, and ask Heaven's blessing on our great content."

So the word went round and the feast was made. The King came to table in the splendid robe he kept for great occasions. It was the color of gold, and round his waist was a golden girdle. On his feet were his jeweled boots, on his head a diadem of gold and jewels. As he entered the hall with Fastrada at his side in regal purple, the musicians struck up and the singers joined with them in a royal greeting. The hall resounded to the splendid clamor of this family occasion.

At the high table sat the King and Fastrada, with Carl and Pepin and Lewis, with Bertha and Rhotrud and Gobbo, who now was never called anything but Pepin the Hunchback to distinguish him from his younger, happier half brother. And Alcuin, the dear and respected friend, his Master's master, as the King so often called him, sat also at the place of honor. He was joined there by the returned Anghilbert, by Arnold who all these years had had the care of Lewis's household. There, too, sat Rotechild, who had cared equally for Pepin of Italy, and his wife, who had been a mother to the boy. And Duke Eric too. And Count Gerold, brother by marriage of the King.

Bertha sat near Anghilbert but hardly spoke or lifted her eyes. Rhotrud was gay, but her heart and her true attention lay elsewhere. Roriko was not at court, he had been bidden home to his own estates; his father had died and now he was Count Roriko of Maine.

On Anghilbert's other side, Carl spoke softly: "What have you done to my brother Lewis?"

"Why?" replied Anghilbert cautiously. "He is well, is he not?"

"He is a pious doll!" said Carl rudely. "I wonder how my father sired such a pomposity!"

"And he was such a pretty baby," Rhotrud sighed, leaning toward them, her dark head close to Bertha's fair one, her eyes darting wickedly toward Lewis, who sat eating nothing, to signify his disapproval of this feast out of festival time.

Anghilbert smiled. On his lean face and in his dark deep-set eyes there was great pity.

"Do not be harsh to him," he said. "What has he known of happiness, poor lad? Truly he is overpious— we all know men may be so. But he is young. He will grow more robust."

"He will not!" declared Rhotrud. "Not with that thin small mouth, Anghilbert. And the conceit of him-self that he wears like a golden halo round his head. Oh if he were only half as merry as Pepin, half as strong as Carl—then he might be well enough."

"He has known no true home, Lady Rhotrud," Anghilbert reminded her in his gentle voice. "And he is still only a child."

"We, too, lost our mother," Bertha said, speaking for the first time. "We have had no true home since."

"Listen," said Anghilbert, turning to her and smil-ing, "here is a tale I will tell you—as I often told you tales in the past. . . . There was once a young prince who inherited a kingdom while he was still just three years old. His kingdom lay far away from the places he knew, where dwelt his brothers and his sisters. They took him from his mother and carried him in a cradle across the mountains, by mighty rivers where the horses had to swim and where men might drown. Through great forests they conducted him, and across open plains. At last, as they came to another great river, they saw ahead of them the city where was the young King's throne, and his palace where he would dwell with none of his own blood about him. Then they took him from the cradle, and the armorers came running with the little suit of armor they had made him, finely and intricately wrought. His nurses and his governors put on the armor and buckled it. At first its stiffness frightened him, but then he strutted like a very small soldier. They lifted him onto a great charger, a mighty war horse, and held a great sword for him, which his small hands clasped about the hilt. The people of the city came running to greet and welcome their King. The men cheered the little warrior and threw their caps in the air for him. But every woman in that great crowd wept to see him."

They were silent when Anghilbert had finished speaking. They looked at the pale, rather spiteful face of their brother Lewis and there seemed nothing they could say.

"It is what men do to children," Anghilbert said, "that makes or mars our world."

Later the musicians played again, and with the board cleared and the logs thrown on the fire so that the flames leaped toward the ceiling, there was dancing down the length of the great hall. Some peasants came first to dance their local dances, then the rest joined in with them. Of the King's family, only Lewis did not dance. Very early, he made his excuses to the King and went away. He would go to the chapel, Arnold explained. The rest felt briefly ashamed that they should be outstripped in good behavior by the youngest brother, and that his piety should seem so tiresome to them. Then they cheerfully forgot him and enjoyed themselves.

They all went late to their beds that night. And barely had the first deep sleep given way to dreams than there was a mighty thundering at the city gates.

"Open!" shouted soldiers' voices. "Open the gates to Witikind the Saxon and his kinsman Abbion!"

VII

Witikind

COUNT AMALWIN, who had been sent to treat with Witikind, produced him now for the King with the air of a man who has conjured up some masterpiece and waits for it to be admired.

In the big chilly chamber where only yesterday the

King had sat to discuss the future of learning in his lands, there now were assembled all of the court who could find a place. The King had not yet entered, nor his old enemy, the Saxon chief. But those seated and standing in the long room, where were gathered many treasures of tapestry and carving, talked eagerly of what was to come from this meeting.

"I would cut his throat," growled one old warrior. It was Eishere of Thurgau, a giant of a man, who complained bitterly of the insignificansce of every enemy he fought. "Why should I be bothered with these tadpoles?" he had been known to cry. "I used sometimes to spit eight or nine of them on my spear and carry them about with me!" So now his fierce-sounding declaration caused only shrugs and laughter.

"The Saxon comes as a guest. Do you cut the throats of your guests, then, Eishere?"

"What a fine fellow you are to be a leigeman of our lord King Charles of the Franks. He has shown courtesy—shall we do less?"

"As there is the matter of our own hostages," the old man conceded, "I will restrain my feelings."

Carl sat with Lewis and Pepin at the right hand of the King's chair. There had been some jostling by Lewis; he was the youngest, he should have taken the lowest place, but he was quite ready to thrust ahead of the others.

"Take your place and be done with shuffling!" Carl said. And he kicked a stool toward Lewis so that it caught him behind the knees and he subsided abruptly. A stifled laugh nearly choked Pepin, and Carl smote him on the back ostentatiously until he had recovered. Carl was delighted with Pepin. This was a brother after his own heart. With the oncoming strength of a worthy son of his father, Pepin had the merry spirits and dark soft eyes of his mother Hildegarde. Looking at the brother they had not seen for so long, the three eldest of her children remembered their mother again and rejoiced; and in Pepin's voice, which sometimes slipped back into a boyish treble, they heard, too, a voice long lost.

Carl looked round the chamber at the counts and the bishops, the clerks and the soldiers. Alcuin and Arnold were disputing gravely together, and on the far side of the archway that led out to the gallery, Bertha sat with Anghilbert at her side. They did not speak very often; but sometimes they would turn and look at one another. It was entirely clear to Carl that if Bertha loved Anghilbert, so too and as deeply did Anghilbert love Bertha. That he was many years older than she was seemed to have no bearing on the case. But Carl felt uneasy none the less. There would be trouble over this business, he was convinced of it. . . .

The seneschal entering and beating upon the floor with his staff of office abruptly silenced the company. All rose. A murmur of anticipation broke the immediate quiet, then died utterly. The whole concourse was still, looking toward the archway through which the King would enter.

The King entered alone and strode to the great

raised chair that was his throne. As the assembled company rose to greet him a breath of speculation moved among them. Where was the Queen at this vital moment of her husband's life? Fastrada, then, did not see fit to greet the barbarian Saxons. There was none there who regretted her absence. Suddenly the whole assembly seemed to take on a different complexion. It became a gathering in which each man there felt himself in union with the King—without the presence of the Queen to separate them. For separate them she did, imposing her own cold will like a sword between King and court.

Charles the King seated himself and called to Amalwin.

"My lord Count, you have conducted strangers to Paderborn. We would speak with them now, since they are willing. I pray you—bring the Saxon chiefs to us here."

"They are already come, Lord King," replied Amalwin.

Then he went to the antechamber and returned with the two men. He spoke to them in their own tongue briefly, and his manner was anxious. Now that he had them here, would they fail him?

Witikind was tall. His fair hair had grayed entirely and his long beard bushed about his chest. He held his head as proudly as any king, and his great shoulders were squared. He wore the rough clothes he had traveled in, with a great studded leather jerkin covering his strong torso. Round his waist was a broad

sword belt, and he had scorned the courtesy of re-
moving his sword, which clanked in its sheath against
his thigh as he crossed the floor and faced the King.

Many years of bitter struggle lay between these
two men, standing now face to face for the first time.
Each had been forced to compromise; the King had
sworn to have Witikind's head and he had failed.
Witkind had defied King Charles to despoil the lands
of the Saxon people, and he too had failed. The lands
were laid waste, the people starving. For their sake
Witikind had set aside his pride and come to the
King at the King's own earnest invitation. He knew
that but for his kinsman, Abbion, who stood at his
elbow, he was alone in an enemy camp, that the man
who faced him and commanded that camp was the
man who had slaughtered thousands of his followers.
Yet he did not falter. Firm and steady he crossed the
open floor in the intense silence. Five or six paces
from the throne he stopped. He folded his arms and
looked the King firmly in the eye.

For a second or two the silence, the long gaze between the two men seemed unbreakable. Then the
King abruptly rose. He came from his chair holding
out both hands in greeting.

For an instant longer Witikind held his stern stillness. Then with a cry that seemed to come more
from his heart than from his throat, it was so deep,
he too flung out both hands. Taking a quick stride
forward, he met the King, and the hands of the two
rulers clasped firmly. Before the eyes of the assembled

court, before the bishops and the counts and the captains, the two who had been such bitter enemies embraced with a sudden overflowing of warmth and mutual respect.

Then indeed the silence was broken, as excited and admiring talk broke out among the witnesses of this reconciliation.

The King seemed to hear nothing of his court's unruliness. He was intent upon Witikind and upon Abbion. He took Witikind by the hand and led him to the place beside the throne where Fastrada should have sat. Then, realizing this still gave him eminence over the Saxon, he called for a stool that he could draw up close by Witikind's. He summoned Alcuin and Anghilbert; he called to Amalwin and shouted for wine that they might all drink together. When the drinking horn was brought, Charles the King drank first and then handed the horn to Witikind, that there might be no thought—as there might be, even now—of treachery, of poison.

Gradually the warmth and the good will, the realization that the King, once set upon his path, would spend himself to outdo his own generosity, worked upon the Saxons so that their grimness relaxed. The halting exchanges between the two great men, aided by Amalwin and Alcuin, became increasingly fluent.

At last the King, his hand still upon Witikind's shoulder, rose and addressed the court.

"This day sees an end of much bitter strife," he cried. "I no longer have an enemy among the Saxons! This I swear in celebration of our understanding: that

the wasted lands shall be ploughed and sown, that the
ravaged villages shall be rebuilt, that health and prosperity shall return. What I have taken away, freely I
give back."

Witikind gave his first, his only smile of bitterness.

"But you cannot, Lord King, give back the lives
you have destroyed."

"This must be my burden as well as the Saxons'."

"And in return for the benefits you speak of?" Witikind asked.

"In return, your fealty—to me as your King. But
more than all this I desire your higher fealty and
that of your people. For though I am a King I too
can bow my knee to my King in Heaven." He made
a sweeping, expansive movement of his arms that
seemed to bring all present within his embrace. "Now
at once we will go to the chapel, and sing *Te Deum*
for this day's great work. And at the altar steps Witikind the Saxon and Charles, King of the Franks,
shall kneel side by side."

From a pace or two away, Carl saw Alcuin watching the King. Alcuin's face wore that affectionate yet
disapproving smile that Carl had so often seen. If
there was a man living who knew Charles through
and through, that man was Alcuin of England. For
a moment it seemed as if he might be going to speak
to the King, to remonstrate with him on this too
strategical attempt at Christianizing the Saxon. Then
Alcuin shrugged very slightly and shook his head.
He turned and smiled at Carl.

"Come, then. We will all sing and pray together.

I daresay Almighty God is the best strategist. In His hands be this day and its doings."

"Amen," said young Lewis.

With a quick glance, one to the other, Carl and Pepin moved off together after the King, across the broad courtyard where the spring sunshine streamed, and so into the familiar quiet and dimness of the chapel.

Witikind remained at court for seven days; and then for seven days more. In that time stern matters were discussed and plans drawn up for the recovery of the Saxon territories. Witikind had not yet given his oath of fealty, nor had he made any comment on the King's further demand that he should accept Christian baptism and carry this faith back with him to his own pagan people. But with the political problems resolved, he seemed still in no hurry to be on his way. It had not been possible for him to refuse that first request—that he should kneel in chapel at the King's side. Yet he must surely have done so with little gladness in his heart; for the man who now urged him to friendship was still the slayer of Witikind's people, still the man who had destroyed the sacred trees and groves where the Saxons worshiped their own gods. And indeed though he bent his knee that first day he did not yet bow his head. With his arms folded he faced the altar proudly still.

But in the days that followed, his manner changed.

"He respects my father for what he has done," Carl

said to Alcuin. "Even the slaughter he will tolerate because it was just." He glanced at Alcuin. "I mean Verden," he said, almost defiantly, as though he himself would seek for the King the absolution he still needed for that day's work.

Alcuin sighed deeply. "Well, who knows—they may not have died in vain. We must pray, Carl—we must all most earnestly pray."

On the sixteenth day of his stay at Paderborn, Witikind, at his own request, swore his loyal oath to the King. He knelt before him, laid his two folded hands within the King's and touched them with his forehead and his lips.

Yet even when this ceremony was accomplished, Witikind lingered. He seemed now to be wrestling with himself, to be fighting his own inclinations. Some said it was his kinsman Abbion who influenced him. And indeed it was Abbion who first sought out Alcuin. Then with the help of Amalwin they spoke together long and deeply and at last Witikind himself came to join them. Carl listened to the disputing in deep admiration of Alcuin's unflagging wisdom and patience and gentle piety.

"It is much for my people to accept that I have bowed the knee to this King," Witikind said. "But if I should return also with a new God—how will they greet me?"

"As their leader still, surely," Alcuin replied. "As their leader strengthened by the Christian faith."

"But if I am strengthened," said Witikind shrewdly,

"how am I also defeated by the King of the Franks?"

"It is the spirit that is strengthened, Lord Witikind."

"But it is a new spirit, one that must not rise in battle. This is something the Saxons will not understand. To them a strong man is strong in body, strong in arm, strong in sword."

"Then it is from you that they must learn," Alcuin insisted, "that strength comes from the soul and the spirit informed by God. Teach them this, my lord. Tell them that from this doctrine a new land and a new people will arise, to live in peace and prosperity under a beneficent rule. Teach them as you now wish to be taught. For I think you wish it."

"It is hard for me too," Witikind replied. "I, too, am a Saxon. It is not in my nature to bow my head."

"Though this must seem a paradox," said Alcuin, "by Christ Himself you shall be strengthened in humility. Submit your will to His and your reward shall be great. For out of this shall come a new dawn, both temporal and spiritual, for your people."

As they sat together disputing, the King himself came to join them.

Witikind gave his old enemy, who was his new friend though admittedly his liege lord too—a long and piercing glance.

"I will accept baptism," he said at last. "I will take this new God home to my people."

Alcuin began to protest anxiously at this conception of Witikind's, but the King delightedly clapped the Saxon about the shoulders.

"I shall myself be your sponsor!" he cried. "This shall be a great occasion—the greatest yet known in my time. Now indeed we may rejoice together, Frank and Saxon alike. God and His wisdom be praised for this mighty blessing!"

Alcuin made no protest. The King's manifest delight moved his friend and teacher deeply. He smiled, though ruefully.

"Perhaps," he said to Carl when they were alone, "I am being foolish. Perhaps when true comprehension comes it will be the stronger for growing slowly. Baptism is a mighty sacrament. It brings its own power to the will. What do you say, Carl? Better any Christian than no Christian? Or better no Christian than a doubtful Christian?"

Carl frowned. "You should ask my brother Lewis. He is the one of us best fitted to dispute on religion."

"I know his reply before he makes it," Alcuin replied. "But I am not convinced it is the right one. . . . God's will be done in this as in all things."

Now that his decision was made, Witikind was eager to receive baptism and be away. Two things delayed him. The first was Alcuin's determination that the Saxon chief should be more fully instructed in the beliefs and laws of the Church he was entering. The second supported Alcuin. Holy Week was upon them. No better occasion for Witikind's baptism could be wished for than the Easter festival.

It was, therefore, when the solemnities had given way to praise and rejoicing, that Witikind the Saxon, together with Abbion, solemnly abjured the beliefs and rites of paganism. As he had promised, the King himself stood sponsor for the Saxon chiefs, and the whole occasion was made one of great and generous festivity.

On that day Charles the King seemed to forget all pomp and majesty. This was the man his children knew most dearly—warm in manner, youthful and gay. His delight in Witikind's conversion overcame all other considerations. He had not the slightest misgiving about the good faith of the Saxon.

"And he is no doubt right enough," Anghilbert said. "They are both sincere today. It is the future we must wonder about a little." He sighed. "Well, we had better be more certain of our own faith, I daresay, before we so lightly question another's. The King is happy and content. He is not always so. We should rejoice in that at least."

Indeed it was a long time since any of them had seen Charles in this carefree mood. It was impossible not to feel that he was released by Fastrada's stubborn absence. Even Gobbo, recently so withdrawn into himself that he seemed hardly a member of the family, came out of his shell when they feasted that day and Witikind and Abbion sat in the seats of honor, one on either side of the King.

Then suddenly the days of festival were past. Witikind and his kinsman rode away. With them went Amalwin, to fetch back the hostages he had left in the Saxon stronghold. In the train, too, went those several clerics who had been appointed as Witikind's advisers and instructors in the new religion.

Pepin, his homage duly made to the King his father, prepared to ride back into Italy. Not a man or a woman there but regretted his departure. He rode off as jauntily as he had come, with a scarlet cap on his dark curls and a promise to his sisters to remember them and send gifts from Italy, which he had quite overlooked on setting out.

Then it was Lewis's turn to go. And he spoke sternly to his sisters before he left. "You are too empty-headed and bedizened," he informed them. "Remember what St. Paul has said."

"What a solemn little poppet, to be sure!" cried Rhotrud, quite forgetting in her annoyance that men honored her by calling her the Dove.

"I'd bedizen the little wretch!" cried Bertha. "I'm glad to see the back of him—whatever Anghilbert may say in his defense!"

Bertha's eyes were shining, her cheeks were red. But it was only in part anger that made her look so vital. She was glowing with exuberant happiness. Pepin was going home with all his train about him as he had come, but Lewis was leaving behind the most important person in the world for Bertha. Alcuin had asked that Anghilbert might remain to take up once more his place in the palace school, where he had been greatly missed. The King was in a mood to grant requests, particularly when they came so near his own. He loved and respected Anghilbert. Perhaps, too, he was not altogether displeased to impose his will on pious Lewis, who seemed so old for his years, so frighteningly self-confident.

Before the last rider in Lewis's train was beyond the gates, Bertha was running to find Anghilbert. . . .

Carl watched her go. He was suddenly seized with a bitter loneliness. He had lost Bertha to Anghilbert now, as he had lost his father to Fastrada. Pepin had gone home and Rhotrud's interest lay away from the court.

There seemed at that moment to be no one in the world to whom Carl might turn for friendship.

VIII

Bertha

IN THE YEARS that followed the submission of
Witikind, life for the King's family and court followed a now familiar pattern. Perhaps for six months
or a year the King would remain passive—too passive, some said, for a mighty warrior whose time had

107

not come when he could afford to rest. Settled comfortably with his family at Aachen or Thionville, Paderborn or Ratisbon, he allowed the greater number of his campaigns to be conducted by his trusted generals, and of these Carl was now one.

There were still savage tribes wandering the wilder parts of Europe and these must be put down. The influence of King Charles of the Franks—Charles the Great, as men were just now beginning to call him—was extended by these small campaigns ably conducted until frontier after frontier fell to his rule. The tide of paganism was being rolled back by the advancing and increasing power of Christian thought. Inevitably there were setbacks and relapses, sudden treacheries, disappointments. But the whole great design moved on its course toward a goal the King, whether active or passive, kept before him like a star. Carl knew what crown his father longed to wear; and he thought that Alcuin knew too. But this was something that was not yet openly spoken of, an ambition so great it still seemed presumption to put it into plain words.

While the King sent his commanders to fight for him, he himself never ceased his vigilant and wise administration. There were synods and diets and councils. Bridges were built across the mighty river Elbe; there were plans for a canal to link the Rhine and the Danube and thus greatly speed transport from place to place. The Church flourished ever in new centers, supported by monasteries and by schools, and there was much building and planning for a new way of life.

About these affairs the King had ridden into Italy, into Brittany, and once to the wild shores of the Baltic; there a new horizon opened up toward which his ambitious eye turned eagerly. On such expeditions nowadays the King went without his wife. Unlike the loving Hildegarde, who had followed her husband wherever he chose to journey, Fastrada, claiming poor health, remained at home. Was this why the King hesitated to be about his own campaigns as frequently as in the past? Some said so. To others, the King's greater employment of delegates trained in his ways seemed most wise, the natural outcome of his years of intense activity in the field. None the less Fastrada kept a court of her own, where flatterers who sought high places knew how best to achieve their purposes.

Increasingly there was a division of opinion, a division of loyalties. When the betrothal of Rhotrud to the young Emperor Constantine was abruptly broken, gossip was quick with the rumor that Fastrada had had a hand in the affair.

"She will not suffer a stepdaughter to become an Empress. She has prevailed upon the King to end the betrothal."

The betrothal in fact was ended at the instigation of the Empress Irene and there was cause for offense. But all the King would say was that he rejoiced.

"For how shall I bear to lose my daughters? How can I ever let my girls go from me? Now Rhotrud shall remain with us always."

It was enough for Rhotrud that the unseen bonds

were broken and she was free. A few months later Count Roriko of Maine came riding back to Aachen, where the family was then settled, and took up a post of honor at the court of King Charles the Great.

Carl was happy for Rhotrud, but he never ceased to be troubled about Bertha.

All this time, no husband had been spoken of for Bertha. She had many suitors but all were turned away. So now Rhotrud, free again, might have seemed an obvious match for the right man. But no such match was hinted at. Why? Did the King intend to restrict the number of his lawful heirs, therefore of claimants to his throne, by denying his daughters marriage? There were those who said so.

The King knew as well as anyone that Bertha loved Anghilbert and had done so from childhood. He did not even ignore the matter, but treated Anghilbert just as he might have done a son-in-law, smiled on the lovers—and laughed when it was suggested they might marry.

"Have you not everything here that you desire, my child? Love and comfort and entertainment, learning and dispute with wise and holy men, sport and good company? Here are your brothers and your sisters, your friends and your servants—and a father who delights in you always."

"Unless I have the husband I choose," said Bertha, "all this counts very little."

"We will speak of it another day."

So it was always; he would always speak of it another day. But the dispute remained the same, and the answer too. Only Bertha changed, hardening in resolution.

Carl had had little time for the kind of dalliance he watched with tolerant amusement in his family and friends. But he knew it was time he thought of marriage. Sometimes when he was returning after months of campaigning to the pleasant life of statecraft and scholarship, music and poetry, sport and easy flirtation, he was amazed by his feeling of loneliness.

A year or so ago an English monk, breaking the long journey home to his monastery, whose business had taken him to Rome, had stayed briefly at the court of King Charles. He had spoken much of his own country, and of King Offa, ruler of the great British kingdom of Mercia.

"But," said the monk, "though his possessions are a thousandfold, none compares with his daughter. For she is as wise as she is beautiful, as brave as she is wise. He who wins her hand wins for himself great treasure."

Carl had heard the praises sung of many ladies; but for some reason he could not name, King Offa's daughter seemed of them all the most desirable. His thoughts of the unknown princess grew stronger, she absorbed his imagination. And often he would find himself repeating what the monk had said: *As wise as she is beautiful, as brave as she is wise. . . .*

Carl returned home one day at the beginning of a wet autumn, after a successful summer in the field, to find Bertha impatiently awaiting him. She was intensely pale, and he saw that since their last meeting she had ceased finally to be a girl and had become a beautiful and strong-willed woman.

"I have been watching for you for days," she said. "He has refused us again. Carl—I have decided not to waste any more of my life. Anghilbert and I plan to wed in secret. Give us your blessing—and your help. For we see no way to manage otherwise!"

It was dark at the foot of the stairs. Carl waited in the shadow of the archway. It was raining and he feared that the guard might choose to shelter for a time in the archway. If Carl was discovered lurking there he would have to think very quickly of some plausible reason.

Bertha had said she would not quit her chamber until Rhotrud slept. To reach the stairway, Bertha had to pass through the room where Rhotrud lay. It was not that she mistrusted her sister, only that she had no desire to involve her in the deception. The fewer people who shared this secret the better.

Carl pulled his dark cloak tighter round his shoulders. The night was not cold but the damp struck into his bones and made him shiver. And perhaps more than the damp. He was already half wishing he had not been fool enough to become involved in this enterprise. Deeply as he sympathized with Bertha and with the devoted Anghilbert, he knew in his heart they were all three being utterly foolhardy. He could think of no one who had chosen to defy the King's wishes in this fashion. None dared, or perhaps none desired to do so. Deeply as he considered the

King's wrath, however, Carl knew that the reckoning would be less with the King himself than with Fastrada, who would be glad to learn of any perfidy committed by Hildegarde's children. . . .

He felt rather than saw Bertha on the stair behind him. She came down so lightly that there was indeed no sound but the soft pull of her cloak against the rough stone of the stairway wall. He thought tenderly how far she had grown from the sturdy little girl who had wanted to follow him to battle.

"I am here," she said in his ear, no more than breathing it.

Carl took her hand and held it hard.

"Think once more, Bertha—think what you're doing. The King has forbidden it. Our own father has forbidden it. Anghilbert is fifteen years or more older than you."

"If he were fifteen years younger than I am—still I should not change."

Carl gave a quick grin. "Except that then he would hardly be worth marrying!"

She tweaked his hair sharply, then put her hand over his mouth to stop him crying out.

"Hush!" he said, pushing her off. He dragged her farther into the shadow. The guard was approaching the entry. When he reached the inviting shelter of the arched doorway, he stepped inside, blowing on his fingers, stamping his feet, muttering to himself. "Holy Mother, if all the winter is to go this way . . . What a night!" Then he rubbed his hands and cried out in pain, for they were numb with cold.

Carl and Bertha remained in the shadow, utterly still, pressing tightly into the darkness where the stairway curled to its end. The guard went on muttering and moaning. He was a young lad and thought, no doubt, of his home, where his mother saved him the best bits of the stew and he had a place by the fire at night.

There were footsteps on the further gallery beyond the archway, above the long ramp that led down to the courtyard.

The young guard jumped to attention, seized his spear and then returned to his regular pacing as the patrolling watchman called the hour.

"Now!" breathed Carl.

He took Bertha's wrist and they darted out of the archway, across the gallery and so to the head of the ramp. Before they could start down the slope, the footsteps of the watchman were sounding along the gallery. Brother and sister turned and fled off to the right. The gallery led round to a second stairway that would take them less directly to the small postern gate in the west wall, beyond which horses should be waiting.

As they ran down the second gallery to the stairs, Carl glanced quickly at Bertha. Her hood had fallen back onto her shoulders, her hair was streaming from a narrow gold fillet. His eyes were now accustomed to the dark and he saw how her face shone with excitement and with a high courage that was lent to her by love. Again he thought: It is time that I, too, got wed. . . .

"We have thrown them off," Bertha said in a breath-less whisper.

Seconds later they were crossing the courtyard and Carl was fumbling with the bolts on the small heavy door. Unexpectedly it swung open.

"Is it you, Lord Carl?"

"We are both here. Are the horses ready?"

"They are waiting under the trees. Mine too," re-plied the man, who was cloaked and hooded. "Shall I ride with you?"

"No—no, go back to your bed and forget what you have done for us. But we will not forget."

"Who is it?" Bertha asked, peering through the darkness.

"It is Einhard, Lady Bertha."

"Einhard . . ."

"Here is your horse now," he said. "I will help you mount."

She put her foot in his cupped hands and was into the saddle.

"Give me your hand," she said, stooping down to him.

Einhard held out his hand and Bertha took it in hers. She pressed it against her cheek.

"God keep you," she said.

"And you, lady."

Then they were away, she and Carl, and Einhard was left behind, standing under the trees, a shadow in the deeper shadow.

They had no more than a mile or two to ride. They were bound for the small wooden church on the outskirts of the nearest settlement, where Anghilbert had a good friend in the priest and could rely on help and discretion. As they rode, the rain began to ease and soon stopped altogether. A warm west wind tore the clouds apart and released a shred of moon. The wind blew soft on their cheeks. The horses sniffed it with pleasure, picking up their feet and settling eagerly to a long strong canter.

The church loomed suddenly out of the dark and the horses had to be pulled in hard or they would have carried their fine rhythmic stride on and on into the night until exhaustion made them drop.

Anghilbert had caught at Bertha's bridle almost before they realized he was there. He lifted her down from the saddle, held her a moment, peering into her upturned face. Then he put his arm round her and hurried her inside, calling to Carl as he went.

Carl tethered the two horses, then followed his sister and Anghilbert into the chapel.

The inside of the chapel, lit only by two small candles and the red eye of the sanctuary lamp, glowed none the less with a warmth of its own. As she stood by the altar rail in that poorly adorned place, Bertha put off her dark cloak and stood at Anghilbert's side in a light green gown. She wore no jewels; not perhaps because she wished to disguise her birth, but because at this moment she knew she needed no adornment but her own happiness.

The priest, an old man with a stooped back and a white tonsured head, took a hand of each of the pair standing before him. His quiet, rather tremulous voice pushed back the silence rather than broke it.

The first light was now standing in the sky, colorless, yet with the depth of a pearl.

"Wait," said the old man to the husband and wife, "and I shall say my first Mass two hours early. Only I have none to serve me."

"Make me your acolyte, Father," Carl said.

The King's daughter knelt by her husband, whose riches were only the riches of a scholar and a poet. The King's son, himself to be a king, knelt on the first of the sanctuary steps. He hoped with all his heart he would remember the responses he had learned as a boy, when he and the other youngsters about the court took their turn at serving Mass, Sunday by Sunday, for a grand array of bishops and archbishops. . . .

When Carl, alone and lonely, rode back to the palace, Einhard was still in hiding under the trees. It was morning now. It would look better, Einhard had thought, if the pair of them returned together through the palace gateway as though Lord Carl had taken a morning ride with Einhard his friend and servant.

"Now they are man and wife," Carl said.

"In good time," replied Einhard. "The King has spoken of sending him away."

"Anghilbert? But he was so glad to have him back from Aquitaine!"

"The King said some days ago that Anghilbert was his choice for Abbot of St. Riquier."

"*Abbot?* But Anghilbert is a scholar, not a churchman—"

"None the less, it has been spoken. Would he be the first layman to be given such a post? But now it will be different," Einhard said comfortably. "We shall not lose him now."

"If we are to keep him, then the truth must be told."

"The King loves his daughter. What is done, is done. All will be well."

Carl looked sideways at his father's little secretary, and his heart warmed to him. It was said that Einhard, too, loved Bertha. He could not have given better proof of that love than in helping her to her marriage. He risked the King's favor, his own livelihood; he lost forever any chance, however slender, of gaining the lady for himself.

"And you, too, Lord Carl," said Einhard, "will soon stand at the altar with your bride."

Carl laughed. "You have chosen me a wife then, Einhard?"

"Have you not heard of the envoys?" Einhard cried.

"What envoys? I know nothing."

"They came at sundown and are lodged with Duke Eric. Tomorrow they are to speak with the King."

"I was out hunting until dusk. And since then," said Carl, grinning rather reluctantly, "I have been occupied."

"They are envoys of Offa, King of Mercia," Einhard said.

For a second Carl was silent. Then he said: "What is their business with the King?"

"They have come to speak of trading between our countries. And to tender you the hand of King Offa's daughter in marriage. Or so the story runs."

Again Carl was silent. His heart had leaped absurdly. He thought wildly about the princess, as brave as she was beautiful, whose nameless ideal had haunted him for so long. King Offa's daughter . . .

IX

King Offa's Daughter

THE ENVOYS from King Offa had brought with them as gifts examples of their country's wares. Wool and furs, a beaten copper vessel of magnificent dimensions, a chased golden chalice, a sword of bronze with a jeweled hilt of antique design. Also a portrait of the princess, his daughter, executed, the envoys said, by a deacon of York who had spent some time at the Mercian court, instructing the King and his family.

The portrait was an illuminated drawing on a scroll of parchment contained within an ornamented cylinder of gold. While the woolens and the furs and the rest of the gifts were presented to the King, along with many protestations of kingly friendship, the golden cylinder, with its contained portrait, was presented to Carl.

Carl took out the parchment and unrolled it slowly. The face of a young girl, crudely enough delineated, stared back at him. He might have grimaced at the flat oval of the face, the great eyes, the high forehead under the little gold crown, and the small curling mouth. But as he gazed at the parchment, the harsh lines of the portrait seemed to melt into the softness of flesh. The large eyes seemed to shine with a steadfast yet a merry light. The mouth quirked up at the corner in a smile. Even the stiff flower she held in one hand seemed to blush and breathe.

With a great gush of happiness, Carl looked up from the portrait into the waiting, anxious faces of the envoys.

"The lady is beautiful," he said.

Then everyone present smiled in a contented fashion.

Later, the King called Carl to his own apartments. They had dined hugely because of the guests, and the King had retired to rest as he liked to do for two hours after eating. He was lying on a low couch and over his knees he had pulled one of the skins brought by the Mercians. He was handling it in appraisal and satisfaction when Carl came in.

"They have fine beasts in their forests on that island," he said. He looked at his son and chuckled suddenly. "And fine women, eh, Carl?"

Carl looked with affection at his father's great frame stretched out there on the couch, at his beard flowing splendidly on his chest and the fineness of his strong hands.

"Is it true that King Offa will give me his daughter?" Carl asked.

"He is eager. And you?"

"Yes," Carl agreed. "I too."

By the window Fastrada was sitting working at a tapestry. She stitched spasmodically. She left the dull and difficult parts to her ladies. One sat there beside her now, silent and subdued as Fastrada's ladies seemed always to be.

"So we are to have barbarians at court," Fastrada said.

"The Mercians do not appear barbarian," the King replied mildly.

"An English princess," said Fastrada, "will be strange to our ways. They are savages there, as everyone knows."

"Is Alcuin a savage?" the King asked.

"Alcuin is a man of God."

"He is also an Englishman, Fastrada. You need not fear King Offa's daughter will be any less couth. Carl is not being offered a princess of the Avars for his wife!"

The Avars were a Mongol race of whose fierceness and savagery terrible tales were told. On a distant plain they dwelt within a fortress called The Ring. Nine concentric rows of fortifications were there, guarding, it was said, great stores of treasure. Many and many a time in the past had the King spoken of making an expedition against the Avars. But lately the enterprises had seemed to slip among other enterprises spoken of but unplanned.

"What do you say, my son?" the King cried now. "Shall we wait until the day the Avars are conquered, and bring you the Khagan's daughter in a golden cage?"

Carl laughed. He had seldom felt more fondly toward his father. He wished that the King were here alone that they might speak privately together. But it was increasingly difficult to detach Fastrada from the King's side. Carl would have liked to tell about his dreams of this princess who had so unexpectedly been offered to him in marriage; how he had heard her spoken of as much as two years ago, and how ever since he had imagined her becoming his wife. . . . To speak of these rather boyish fantasies was impossible in Fastrada's presence.

So he could only say: "I will have Offa's daughter, if that pleases you, my lord."

"I think it pleases me," his father answered. He put out his hand, took Carl by the wrist and gave him a hard warm pressure. "We will send the envoys back with tidings that should please them all. It is time we had a marriage in this family—it is high time."

The thought of Bertha stabbed at Carl's conscience. He felt a traitor to his father. And again he was deeply moved by the thought of trouble to come.

There was, in fact, trouble the following day.

Summoned before the King, the envoys of King Offa received with respectful pleasure the news that the King of the Franks accepted the English King's daughter for his son.

Carl stood beside his father's chair when the acceptance was made. He could not tell what he felt as the Mercians turned to him and bowed deeply.

"This is an honor for our master's daughter," said one.

"But a joy, too, for the Lord Carl," said a second. "The lady is beautiful and she sings as a bird sings. She is forever busy about her womanly concerns. She stitches finely, embroiders well. Her voice is merry and she laughs often. Blessed be your days with her, young Lord Carl. Blessed be hers with you and with your children."

"Blessed indeed," replied the chief spokesman among them. "And if, to help the lady's impatience, we may bear back with us a likeness . . ."

Carl laughed. "I am a soldier, Englishman. Who makes likenesses of soldiers save only God?"

"We will make a likeness with words," said the man from Mercia. "How tall, how keen of eye, how strong of voice and purpose, how devout. How skilled in battle, how apt in learning. How fine a son to make as fine a husband."

Carl held up his hands in protest and alarm. "If you make me out a giant, a saint and a scholar—how shall I stop her tears when she sees me as I am?"

In celebration of a piece of business well concluded, the King called for wine. The King drank to his fellow King, Offa of Mercia, and to the daughter-in-law he had willingly accepted. The envoys drank also to their own master, then to their young princess's future husband. Carl drank to the wife who would one day be his. Good will flowed and overflowed, no embassy could have reached a more amicable conclusion.

"For the rest of our embassy," the leader of the Mercians now said, "we have also a happy proposal to make in the name of our King. He, too, has a son. That son is his heir and will one day be King of Mercia. And that son, our young Prince, also seeks a wife. It is the earnest hope of our master, Lord King, that you will vouchsafe your daughter the Lady Bertha as a wife for King Offa's son and heir."

Carl felt his face stiffen. He glanced in panic from his father to his father's secretary. Only Einhard in that gathering could know how dangerous a moment this was.

The King's face, too, had changed from its friendliness and condescension to a cautious watchfulness.

"Daughter for daughter?" he asked. "Is this what King Offa intends?"

"It is to be a mutual happiness," the envoy murmured.

"Is it indeed so?" the King said, with a short laugh. "I am to give my daughter as a hostage for his? Is that his meaning?"

"Hostage is no word to use, one King to another!"

"It is the word I use," King Charles replied. "As would any other man of sense. What do you say, Carl?"

"It is not likely that my sister would care to leave her home so far behind," Carl said cautiously.

"Nor would I send her so far."

"It is the same distance, Lord King, as our master will send his daughter for your son."

"It is not to be thought of."

The envoys looked at one another uneasily, and excusing themselves they moved together momentarily and spoke in low voices in their own tongue. The smiles had given way to anxious frowns; the whispering, though neither Carl nor the King himself could follow what was being said, was palpably agitated.

Einhard sat looking from Carl to the King, from the King to the envoys. At this purely state conference, Fastrada was not present.

Carl turned his back on Einhard and tried to straighten and order his own thoughts. In his heart he had known that the negotiations were going too smoothly. Deep impatience stirred in him. He wanted this princess for his own and that there should be delay or anger over the terms on which he obtained her filled him with rage and helplessness.

At last the spokesman of the four envoys addressed himself again to the King.

"My lord—may not the lady be consulted?"

The King laughed. "It is a foolhardy father who allows his daughters to choose the men they fancy. He can at least protect them from their own folly! A girl may love where she pleases, but to her own danger. It is by no means certain that her hand can in good sense be allowed to follow her heart."

"Then we must say this to our master: King Charles of the Franks finds himself unable to accept the marriage offers."

Carl tried to tell himself he was happy that Bertha had been saved the disclosure of her marriage with Anghilbert. He loved his sister and wished nothing but good to her. But his anxiety on his own account changed at this moment to despair.

"You must say to your master," replied King Charles, "that I do not part easily with my daughters. But they shall welcome his as a sister among them."

"Alas," said the envoy, "that cannot be. It is expressly stated in our embassy that the one must depend upon the other. For, my Lord, why should one prince be granted a bride when the other is denied his choice?"

"We, too, will echo that *Alas!*" said the King. "But we cannot find a word we would all prefer." He rose and the rest rose with him. "The audience is ended," he said. He put out his hand to Carl, who moved toward him. With his hand on the arm of his eldest son, and without a backward glance, King Charles of the Franks quitted the envoys sent so hopefully from so far.

Once out of earshot, striding down the gallery to his own apartments, the King laughed.

"Carl, you look very sour! Forgive me—but this is nothing—there are hundreds of ladies as beautiful, as sensible, and no doubt with as birdlike voices. . . . Come, you must rally—I have seldom seen you so glum. It will not be difficult to find you a lovely and loving wife. Or at least," he added, with a flare of anger, "not if you look like a man instead of a sullen schoolboy!"

He turned away abruptly, to rejoin Fastrada, who would nod her head in a knowing way. "Did I not say this was a barbarian king of a barbarian court? Not to trust his daughter here! Heaven save us from all such monsters!" But her true satisfaction would be in the discomfiture of the King's heir.

Carl returned the way he had come, unable even to remonstrate with his father in his own cause. He felt sick with disappointment. He could hardly believe that his promised happiness had been snatched away from him so abruptly and so soon. In vain he told himself that all reports might lie, that the girl might in fact be squat and ill-tempered, squint-eyed, and violent of mood. . . .

As he wrestled with his feeling of terrible frustration and wretchedness, Carl saw his brother Gobbo moving away down a far stairway with three or four of the young men who had recently formed themselves into a group about him, making him a little court and a following of his own; they were the sons, without exception, of men who had first come to court in attendence on Gobbo's mother, the King's first wife.

Moving away in a group as they were now doing, they gave the impression of being partners in some enterprise, one which they intended to be secret. They spoke to one another in low voices, then looked quickly round as though they might have been overheard.

Carl shrugged impatiently. His own troubles filled his mind, he could not be bothered now with whatever mischief Gobbo might be up to. . . .

He went to his bedchamber and lay on his bed. If he were Rhotrud, he thought, he would pray and find relief. If he were Lewis he would be kneeling in the chapel with his grief. If he were Pepin he would no doubt be about the business of seeking another bride as quickly as possible. Instead he lay moaning in wretchedness on his bed.

Hard as he tried, he was unable to pray, unable to drag himself to his feet. All his efforts at gaining the same iron firmness as his father had now vanished into nothingness. He was pinned down by his loneliness, by the feeling that he was less a son to his father than a pawn in the game of politics and power that was being played out in Europe. He knew in his heart that more than politics and temporal power were involved. But in the bitterness and sadness of his thought at this moment he saw only what blunders his father might have made as he moved toward his great objective. He remembered Verden and the massacre of the Saxons, the lands laid waste, the outcry of those wretched people who had been shifted from their homes because they had revolted against the Frankish rule, or against Christianity; he thought how they had been transported and resettled by the thousands in territories they did not know, which they must colonize or perish. . . . He forgot the schools and the churches, the new just laws that took account of things till now ignored; the pleasant home life of learning and music and sport; the exaltation of the Church; the respect and affection of Pope Hadrian for this mighty King. Carl knew his father wise and just, he loved him with all his heart even though Fastrada had raised a barrier between them. But all that concerned him now was a young man's sad and bitter disappointment at the loss of his lady. . . .

His servant came in and stood awkwardly, astounded to find him lolling there on his bed.

"It is a message from the Mercian envoys, Lord Carl. They return at once to their own country. They ask for the portrait of the princess."

"Take it!" Carl cried. But as the man took up the portrait Carl checked him. "No—wait. Give it to me."

He unrolled the parchment. He looked again and for the last time at the small proud head with its golden diadem, at the wide brown eyes, the curling mouth, the flower. He waited for the face to live as it had seemed to live before. But it remained flat and withdrawn; a portrait of a remote princess who would never draw closer to him now.

X

The Traitor

A MIGHTY hammering on the door roused Carl
from heavy sleep. He was recently back from the
long promised expedition against the Avars, worn out
with conflict and hard-going and by the fact that although a beginning had been made against these people, it had not, after all, amounted to very much. The
horses had sickened unaccountably, the disease ran

like wildfire through their ranks. It had been necessary to retreat as far as Regensburg on the Danube,
where the court had been moved. There they would
winter, and there now Carl was roused from his sleep
by knocking and shouting. . . .

He came out of confused dreams at last and sprang
up in alarm. His first thought was that the Avars, by
some genius, had re-formed, joined with their main
army and, winter or no, swept across the great Pan-
nonian plain by the Vistula, the Oder and the Elbe,
and so come to the Danubian shore. He pulled on
a robe and snatched up his sword. Then he ran outside to find a stirring everywhere.

"Is it an attack?" he shouted to the nearest guard.

"No one knows, Lord Carl. There is a great noise
at the King's door!"

By this time others were running toward the sound
of the commotion, and by the time Carl reached his
father's quarters he had to thrust his way through
an excited throng. From the King's sleeping chamber
could be heard loud protests and anxious cries.

"Let me pass!" Carl cried to those who stood in
his way.

The King was on his feet with a great fur rug pulled
round him. A man crouched on the floor before him.
Carl recognized him at once as Fardulph, the deacon,
a decent if rather foolish fellow who held a minor cleri-
cal post under Einhard.

"This I heard with my own ears, Lord King!" he
was saying. "With my own ears I heard and was made
to vow silence!"

"And this vow you come to me to break?"

"They took my word violently. I cannot be bound by such an extortion. They threatened me, my lord."

"I marvel—if this is true—that they let you live. . . ." He took Fardulph by the shoulders and stared into his face. "Bring me a light here!"he roared.

Someone ran with a torch and held it, and the King stared closely into the eyes of the man before him.

Suddenly Fardulph, who had seemed to be groveling there, was filled with a strange dignity. "Put out my eyes, if you will! Pluck out my tongue! I swear that I speak truth of what I have heard! I swear by Almighty God, and by His Blessed Mother, that I have no care for my own life. It is my King I come to save!"

The King released him roughly. Then, as though regretting his own savagery, he put his hand again on Fardulph's shoulder and let it rest there a moment.

"Come," he said. "Sit beside me. Tell me again what you have heard."

Carl frowned in bewilderment. "Are we besieged? I thought at least there was an enemy at the gate."

"No." The King shook his head slowly, as though it held now a weight too great to bear. "A traitor within." He turned to Fardulph. "Now tell me again, and slowly. If you gabble so I cannot hear more than a word in every ten."

"I had to gain your ear, my lord. None else would listen. I had to batter my way to your side."

"And a fine state the household is thrown into now!" the King said with a wan smile. "My wife and her women frightened halfway to their deaths and the guards all supposing you meant to murder me in my bed. You are fortunate they did not kill you in their anxiety."

"I would make less noise if I came to harm you—I would move and speak secretly. As *they* have done."

Carl cried, startled: "A conspiracy?"

Fardulph turned to him eagerly. "Yes, Lord Carl—a conspiracy. A bitter conspiracy . . . They met in St. Peter's church nearby. I have seen them entering often. But this night I went there first and hid myself. I hid beneath the altar—may God forgive me any sacrilege. There I lay, and they entered as usual, and close by the altar steps they talked together in low voices. How they would depose and kill the King and set another in his place."

"Another? Who?"

As he spoke, Carl saw his father's eyes dark with pain.

"Who would be king, Fardulph?" he insisted.

"Your brother, Lord Carl. Pepin the Hunchback . . ."

Carl had known in his heart before Fardulph spoke. He had known all along that Gobbo was too much involved with men who could lead him into dangerous mischief. He dared not look at the King again. Fardulph was gabbling on, then checking himself and speaking more slowly. He was naming the conspirators who had met there in the church at midnight to lay their plans. But Carl had no care for any name but one. He knew then most certainly what his conscience had often naggingly suggested—that between them all they had forced Gobbo into a traitor's role.

"Then by wretched misfortune," Fardulph was saying, "I sneezed. 'It is a rat!' cried one. 'A rat that sneezes?' cried another. 'It is a man!' They drew their swords and searched and since they are men who do not fear to violate the sanctuary, they dragged me from my hiding place. They set a dagger at my throat till I vowed I would be silent. Then they left the church and shot the bolts and I was left inside. I feared greatly. I feared they might fire the church. . . . But they went away and left me. I found myself a chink I could escape through—by the ninth step of the belfry. I jumped down and came at once to warn the King."

The King put his hand on the deacon's arm.

"You have done well," he said. "I cannot praise you as I should. For you bring vile tidings."

Then various of the men who had crowded into the bedchamber, standing many of them with swords or daggers that they had snatched up in alarm, urged the King to seize the traitors instantly.

"Yes, yes—I will do so. Leave me now. Leave me."

"It is best not to dally," Carl said grimly.

"Leave me, Carl—go with the rest! He is only half your brother—he is all my son. . . . Leave me! Go!"

"But the command must be given," Carl insisted. "Say only—'These men are to be apprehended.' "

"These men—" the King began. He turned away as though he must hide his face.

"Yes, Father?" Carl said gently. "These men—?"

"These men are to be apprehended and brought before me," the King said with sudden firmness. "See to it, Carl."

Carl left the King's bedchamber, driving the rest before him and snapping out his orders as he went.

He knew that the King had fallen on his knees and that he was weeping.

The trial of his half brother, Gobbo, and those who had conspired with him against the King was an occasion which Carl would spend the rest of his life trying to forget. It was a fact that the King had for some time now inclined to clemency in sentencing criminals, and avoided the death penalty where possible. It was as though he set each life thus spared against those he had destroyed that bitter day at Verden. When the conspirators were arrested, two of them drew their swords and in the affray that followed they were killed. The rest were spared by the King's command. And Einhard commended his master's great generosity, while others grumbled at it.

Carl was uncertain what he felt about the men who had used Gobbo as their tool. Perhaps because he was accustomed to battle and swift death, he thought in his heart that a clean end might be more merciful than the severest punishments the law decreed. Such punishments were meted out to Gobbo's confederates who were in fact his destroyers.

For Gobbo himself there was of necessity a different fate to be decided. He was the King's son and the brother of kings. He had been the sport of circumstance since his birth. The crooked back which had made his mother weep and the unthinking world give him a mocking nickname had lost him, too, his birthright. And because as a child he had been weakly, the other children had shouldered him out. He had always been lonely. That his father had disinherited him and even deprived him of his name had set a seal upon that loneliness and caused him to seek companionship wherever it was to be found—among the toadies who enjoyed favors; among those who thought the King had treated Gobbo and his mother before him harshly and unfairly; among malcontents and those who sought to redress real or imaginary wrongs.

"We are all to blame for his treachery," Carl told Alcuin wearily. He was sick of the business, wrung with misery at the sight of Gobbo now that his plotting had been discovered. "Alcuin—speak to the King! Pray him to be lenient, Alcuin!"

"I will pray *for* him," Alcuin replied.

Suddenly he looked an old man. Carl knew that this dearest friend of them all wanted to leave the court and retire to some monastery to end his days undisturbed. He had spoken of it often, but the King would not listen, he could not tolerate the thought of losing his friend and teacher, the inspiration of all who passed through the palace school.

"I am very much afraid of my stepmother's influence in this matter," Carl insisted. "She is at the root of all unrests. Once, even I—" But he broke off and decided that even now he could not speak of the attempt that had once been made to seduce him from his loyalty. "My father has not been his true self since he married Fastrada. Because of her it may go hard with Gobbo."

Alcuin did not reply. He was not prepared to censure anyone. His very silence rebuked Carl's easy accusations.

"It is true," Carl muttered defensively. "She has kept him at her side and because he has dallied, much ground has been lost. He is great—but without her he could be greater. He should not rest! Do you know there is some talk now of a new Saxon rising?"

Disaster as it must be, even this was less concern to Carl than the unknown fate of his half brother. Gobbo was a prisoner in his own quarters with a guard at every door. Not even Carl had been allowed to visit him. But he had seen him, a day or two after his arrest, staring down from the window slit. His eyes, enormous and unwinking in his handsome death-pale face, had seemed to accuse the entire world.

And that same night he had heard Fastrada say: "He should die! He should die for his treason!"

"It needs a monster to destroy his own child," the King replied.

"It needs only a strong man."

The King had shaken his head and sighed. "I destroyed him long ago," he said. "When I took his name from him, and his true place in the world. Yet I know that when I did so—I did right."

"If you are weak now, you will suffer!"

"I have sometimes been strong—and suffered," he replied.

Carl had only once before seen such unbearable sadness on his father's face; years ago when they were crossing the Jupitersberg, and he had confided to the boy Carl what he intended for Gobbo.

In those long nervous days of waiting for the King's judgment on their half brother, Carl and Bertha and Rhotrud drew together, they were as close as they had been in childhood. It was as though Bertha had never known Anghilbert, or Rhotrud the dashing young Roriko; as though Carl had never dreamed of an unknown princess for whom there was still no successor. They were children again, waiting fearfully for the punishment of some prank—only this time the prank was not a childish one.

It was not until the tenth day after the discovery of the plot, when the confederates had been punished and driven from court, that the King spoke his will in the matter of his eldest son.

Bertha heard it first.

"He will be banished!" she cried to Carl and Rhotrud. "It has all been settled during these last days."

"Banished? Where? And for how long?" Rhotrud cried.

"For always—for all his life!" Bertha answered. She covered her face with her hands and her tears ran between her fingers. "Why have we allowed this to happen to him? Why have we neglected him—so that he had to make friends of evil men?"

"Where is he to be sent?" Carl asked.

"To Prum!"

"The monastery! It is very just. Once he spoke of entering the monastic life. . . ."

"He will be publicly tonsured!" Bertha cried.

Carl felt a chill, brief shiver touch his spine. Whatever Gobbo did, wherever he took his way, he did so as privately as was possible. He would never walk down the middle of the floor if he could make his way along the shelter of the wall. When he rode out, his tallest followers rode close around him, as a shield against prying eyes.

Now he was to start his punishment with a public humiliation. It was indeed fair that the King should send Gobbo to a monastery, for there he would have time for thought and prayer that might help and sustain him. But he must enter behind the high monastic walls, not as a lay prisoner, but as a professed monk whose own vows would hold him forever bound. He must make his act of penitence publicly and before them all have the crown of his head shaved in humility.

This was not the hand of the King and they all knew it.

"It was she who planned it!" Carl cried savagely. "It was a bitter day for all of us when the King married Fastrada! All these years she has held him enslaved. I wish they might never have met—I wish her mother had never borne her!"

"Oh hush, Carl!" Rhotrud cried—as she would have done years ago when they were children, and she was so prim and severe with the rest of them.

"It is madness to judge him—madness to speak against him! We should rather stay close at his side to show him we are still his children—the children of Hildegarde. Truly I think this punishment may send Gobbo mad. But it is too late now to wring our hands. We can only pray for him, poor lad. Who knows—maybe he is destined for great things in the Church—and this will lead him to his true vocation."

"You could always console yourself with pieties, Rhotrud," Bertha said bitterly.

"How else am I to console myself—or any of us? You are cruel, Bertha!"

"Oh peace—for pity's sake!" Carl cried. "I will go to the King and ask that we may all be together with Gobbo for a little time before he leaves us."

The King refused and would not be shaken. The sentence took its course unhindered by any last minute thoughts of compassion. A few days later, without farewells, Gobbo rode away towards Prum in the company of the Master of Novices and three brothers who had been sent to fetch him. A guard of thirty armed men went with them. Gobbo wore the rough robes of the Order he was entering, and a round cap covered the shaven crown of his head, which had been bowed in forced penitence and humility before the King and the whole court. . . .

Whatever Alcuin thought of the King's justice in this matter was spoken only between the two of them, never aloud. But everyone knew that he had been closeted with the King for two hours on the evening the sentence was pronounced. The King's angry voice had frightened those who heard it from outside.

After Gobbo's departure King Charles withdrew himself from the court for ten days and more. When he emerged to deal with matters of state that clamored for attention there was no sign in his face or in his manner that he had suffered any conflict. He had had a son they nicknamed Gobbo; he was gone and would be spoken of no more.

As though to console himself for the defection of one son, the King awarded new honors to the next.

"Why need you wait until my death to wear a crown?" he said to Carl. "Your younger brothers are kings already. Shall you be less than they?"

Then he named Carl, his eldest son and his heir, as King of Neustria.

Carl was glad his father honored him, it spoke of confidence that had once or twice lately seemed withdrawn. But the crown and the ceremony that conferred it seemed to him symbols of a splendor that did not fit him as a soldier. A quarter of his father's dominions now came under his control, reaching northwest to the narrow waters separating the Frankish lands from Britain; and southwest to the frontiers of Aquitaine, where young Lewis ruled; and eastward to the mighty river Scheldt.

Carl traveled this great kingdom, receiving homage from many, and knowing that for the first time he was acting, not as his father's deputy, but as himself.

At home a deep and dangerous slackness seemed to settle over Charles the King. For months he lingered at Regensburg, while Fastrada kept much to her own chamber, even to her bed. She seemed to be ailing as she had often claimed to be, but the cause of her sickness could not be discovered.

In the autumn the canal the King had planned to link the Rhine and Danube had to be abandoned. The ground was marshy, the season appallingly wet, the engineering problems, after all, too great.

The disappointment enraged the King. His temper had never been so short and those nearest to him suffered most. He had never accepted Bertha's marriage to Anghilbert, though it had long been an open secret. He would see them together with their three-year-old son and behave as though the child was not there at all; for a man so devoted to children this was stern discipline. Now at last he made an appointment long spoken of: Anghilbert was to be Abbot of the monastery of St. Riquier. True, Anghilbert would still be at court frequently, as were other men and women with high appointments, largely administrative, at monasteries and convents throughout the King's realms. But long separations were inevitable, not likely to be easily endured by Bertha, whose headstrong temperament was so like her father's.

Then came news confirming the long threatened revolt in Saxony. Barely was this blow digested than a sweating and exhausted courier arrived with word that the Moors had made a raid on Frankish territory and retired unscathed after inflicting heavy casualties.

At last the King stirred. The defection of Witikind, whose conversion had seemed so splendid a triumph, the memory of Roland and the defeat at Roncesvalles that came with the news of the Moorish attack, roused him to action. Perhaps with more doggedness than with the old vigor and energy, he planned his campaign. He would base himself at Frankfurt. And there in the spring the court and the army shifted to prepare an offensive.

Since the entire household was moved, Fastrada went too. Still far from well, she made the journey by easy stages. But as if to punish him for what she called his brutal disregard of her illness and her expressed wishes, she sickened again suddenly.

It was spring. A week or two later, Fastrada died. . . .

Was it indeed an evil enchantment that was removed then from King Charles of the Franks? Or was it his desire to forget his own sorrow, so obviously unshared, that caused him to hurl himself into the planning of the new campaign?

With mighty forces he crossed the Rhine, having appointed a rendezvous with Carl at the head of a second great army. The force was so enormous and so imposing that when the rebels realized against what they were pitted, they threw down their weapons and surrendered.

It might not have been surprising if the King, already tired of broken promises, had dismissed his more clement impulses, acted in violence and slaughtered his treacherous enemies. Instead he treated with them. And he and Carl, King of Neustria, accepted the surrender mercifully.

With Saxon hostages in their train, the two kings, triumphant, rode back across Germany to Aachen.

The summer had spent itself in the course of the campaign and its planning. Soon now it would be autumn and in these shortening days the King of the Franks came once more to his favorite dwelling place. The palace he had built himself welcomed him for the long, inactive winter. His family would be there with him and they would revive the old carefree ways which somehow had lost their savor during the last years.

As he came into the great hall of the palace and moved toward his own apartments, the King saw three ladies, who had been about the court while Fastrada lived, walk down the long gallery talking and laughing together. One he recognized at once: Liutgarda of Allemania, whose gentle laughter seemed to him the most pleasant sound he had heard for many months.

Perhaps, in due time, he might find some way to solace the loneliness he felt without a wife to comfort him.

XI

Emperor?

IT WAS DUKE Eric, the King's old and reliable friend and adviser, who made the first true conquest of the Avars. He it was who broke the famed fortifications of the Ring, with its terrible palisades of thorn, and rode back to Charles the Great bearing loads of

fabulous treasure. With him on this triumphal homeward journey rode the Tudun, an Avarian ruler, who
came to make submission to the King and to ask for
Christian baptism.

Only a year had passed since the death of Fastrada but that year had seen great changes. Now indeed it did seem as though everything that had been
spoken of her was true. If the King had been under
an enchantment he rose from it like a lion uncaged
to rage and roar about his world with all the vigor
of his younger days. And with twice the power. For
now he knew how he must control his anger, how
to win men by trusting them, how to conserve his
forces, how to guard against treachery.

Duke Eric rode back through the deep winter to
the palace at Aachen with great trains of packhorses
carrying treasure. The family had assembled for the
Christmas festival and they were still together. The
welcome given to the duke and his men could hardly
have been louder or warmer or more admiring.

"I should have been there!" the King cried. "Why
was I not there with you, Eric?"

"It would have been a greater triumph for us all,"
Duke Eric said generously. "But tell us we have done
well in your behalf, for it was hard going."

"Truly you have done well!" the King cried.

Then in the great hall, with the fire of huge
branches leaping and blazing, in the glare of torches
which filled the air with light and smoke and the
smell of resin, the treasures were tumbled out before
the King.

Great rubies, golden vessels studded with sapphires, emerald ornaments; chains of beaten silver and bracelets encrusted with amethyst and turquoise; platters of copper, traced and beaten; strings of ivory, great masses of amber and jade; fantastic weapons, with carved and jeweled hilts; shields of silver; drinking vessels of polished horn; furs and silks and embroideries made with threads of gold and silver. The stored plunder from a hundred kingdoms, now plundered in its turn, was poured into the lap of King Charles of the Franks as he sat with his family and his court gathered about him.

With each new marvel as it came to light the cries of wonder grew, while those who had brought home these riches looked on in satisfaction and delight in their own prowess, that the King could not praise too highly.

Then the King began to laugh with pure pleasure himself, and he pulled gems like plums from the ever increasing mound that winked and gleamed in the torchlight and the light of the fire.

"Here, Rhotrud—take this ring! Bertha—the pearl is yours. Carl—yours the chains, the golden chains with the ruby clasp. Lewis shall have the chalice with emeralds. Pepin—here, take these for your wife when you choose her. Where are the children? Theodrada—Himiltrude—come to me here. Choose what you will of these enormous toys! And Liutgarda—come, give me your hand. The greatest prize for you!"

Liutgarda moved forward laughing. She was fair and comfortable and modest. She was, in fact, the

new stepmother whom every one of the family—
save perhaps Lewis—already loved. The King had to
have a woman by his side, he was lost without—
whatever austere Lewis of Aquitaine might say in
disapproval. This time his choice could not have been
a happier one. Now as she stooped her head and he
placed a little crown of gold and rubies on her shining hair, a murmur of pleasure and approval went
round the gathering. Rhotrud, close beside her, leaned
forward and kissed Liutgarda's cheek. Smiling, Bertha touched her hand. Pepin put his arm about her
waist and gave her a quick, warm embrace.

It made Carl laugh aloud to see his father, surrounded by his family, tossing the treasure about, en-
joying himself so hugely. Now they were all friends
again, as closely knit as any laborer's family crowded
into a cottage.

With the family gifts dispensed, the King made fair
division among the men who had carried it home.
None was forgotten, least of all the widows of those
who had not returned.

Now the King was choosing for Alcuin, no longer
at court. He had gone to be Abbot of the great monastery of St. Martin at Tours, and there, he said, he
would stay to await the final "knocking on the gate."

The King set aside piece after piece of splendid
plate.

"This I shall send to Pope Hadrian. And it shall
be an earnest for the soul of the Tudun, who now
seeks baptism." He looked round him rather as he
looked round the table when he had not decided

who should read aloud to them while they dined, "I need a trusted ambassador. It shall be Anghilbert. They must spare you from St. Riquier, Anghilbert, while you make the journey to Rome."

Anghilbert bowed and smiled faintly. He glanced at Bertha. Even in this mellow mood of his the King still plotted to separate these two who had dared to become husband and wife against his wishes.

When he had decided that Anghilbert should be his ambassador to Pope Hadrian, the King began tumbling the treasure back into the chests and bales it had been carried in. At the last he suddenly seized hold of a silver dish.

"I have given nothing to my Dwarfling! Here, Einhard—take this and remember me."

The King embraced his one-time secretary, now near to being his chancellor, and everyone crowded round to look at the silver dish Einhard held tenderly in both hands.

"Our father is a great man," Carl said to Lewis, who was standing by his side. "God keep him so—he is a happy man too." He looked at his brother and saw the austere thin face wearing an expression of pale disapproval. "What now, Lewis?"

"There is too much luxury and love of splendor. I would sweep the place clean of it, if I were King in this palace."

"Sweep your own palace clean!" snapped Carl. "And heaven send that you marry a woman who will turn you into a *human,* not only a *man.*"

Lewis did not reply, but he gave a slight contemptuous smile. He looked across to where Count Ingre's daughter, Irmingarde, sat with a dozen or more ladies. Then he smiled again, a shade more warmly. And Irmingarde smiled back.

"Poor foolish girl," Carl said to Bertha later that evening. "She sits waiting for his glance to fall on her. I would need a finer prize than to be Queen of Aquitaine before I would marry my brother Lewis!"

"She is a silly sheep and deserves all she may get," replied Bertha shortly.

"Rhotrud tells me she is a pious girl."

"She prays a great deal," Bertha admitted. "But I always think her prayers must be directed all to one end—that she may be a king's wife!"

With the enormous sensation of the Avar treasure and the plans for its distribution, the Christmas season came to an end. The brothers began making arrangements to return to their kingdoms. For Carl, too, there were plans that would take him from home; and although he had his kingdom now and must set about its management, this would always be home to him. Pepin and Lewis, however welcome, must always be visitors, and this seemed both sad and strange to Carl. His father remained a hero to him, no less loved, no less admired because he knew that hero's human faults and failings. He knew, too, the strange, unpredictable humility with which the hero so often strove to remedy those faults. That a man could be a giant before men and a suppliant before God seemed to Carl, as it might well do, to be the very pinnacle of human behavior.

Anghilbert's embassy to Pope Hadrian was on the point of setting out for Rome when news came by courier that kept him at home after all.

"On Christmas Day, my lord King," said the courier, standing before Charles, "His Holiness departed this life and entered into the Kingdom of God."

The King cried out in bitter sorrow. Pope Hadrian had been to him not only the Sovereign Pontiff, the Vicar of Christ, the Bishop of Rome—but also a man who knew how to be a friend. Charles turned aside and wept for this friend, and those who were with him at the time stayed silent. They respected his grief, were moved by its sincerity to a depth of sympathy they were unable to express.

Now Pope Leo III sat on the throne of St. Peter.

This might greatly affect the future, as Charles knew well enough. He set aside his sorrow for the dead Hadrian to consider where he stood. Though he had never, in all these years, spoken to anyone but Carl of his highest ambition, it had become an open secret. There were hints from time to time, encouragements. Carl thought often of the day when his father would stand at the head of a new Roman Empire. So splendid a climax would be suited to a career which, in spite of many setbacks, had already been fabulous.

Only one thing had stood between the King's hope and its possibility of fulfillment. Now quite suddenly there might be two obstacles to overcome. The first and most obvious was the fact that the young Emperor Constantine had now come of age and sat on the imperial throne. The second was that Pope Hadrian's death left the King no absolute certainty of support from Rome. He did not know Pope Leo. Would he be a supporter or an opposer of the plan should it ever come to the point of open discussion?

At the Feast of St. Michael, Alcuin sent a set of verses from Tours to his friend and monarch:

> *Michael, Archangel*
> *Of the King of Kings,*
> *Give ear to our voices.*
>
> *We acknowledge thee to be the Prince*
> *of the citizens of Heaven;*
>
> *And at thy prayer God sends*
> *His angels unto man . . .*

The verses ran on, steady and splendid, prayer and poem in one. And at the foot of the manuscript Alcuin had written in his own hand: "Emperor, thy scholar made these melodies for thee."

The manuscript was handed about among those who were able to read it. The word *Emperor* was suddenly heard on the lips of those about the court; whispered, but whispered firmly. A new feeling of excitement, of striving toward a future glorious and powerful in which they might take their humble part, inspired those about the King at that time. There was a mounting tension, though how this thing might be accomplished none could know and none dared ask. The right of the Emperor Constantine to the imperial throne was well established; the right of Charles the Great was the right of achievement, worth, faith and power. It remained to be seen which would prevail.

There were envoys waiting at Aachen when the King rode back to winter quarters after a summer campaign that had proved outstandingly successful.

"They are sent from the Empress Irene," Einhard told the King.

Charles was tired but content at this homecoming. The long years of planning and re-establishing among the tribes and races in Europe were beginning to bear fruit. The conquered people now fought on the Frankish side, the King's forces had become enormous. If he had been able to find fodder for a large enough body of horse he would have continued his campaign that year after the weather broke.

But this was not practicable. So he returned to Aachen to one of those family winters he enjoyed so well. He was fifty-six that year, the last but one of the old century. A moment of pause and portent and nameless promise . . .

The King looked critically at Einhard.

"How pale you are. You are not sickening, Dwarfling?"

Einhard shook his head. "Not bodily, my lord. There is a sickness in my thoughts. For I have spoken with the envoys."

Carl found his father and Einhard together.

"Let them speak for themselves," Einhard was saying. "Do not ask me to report their tidings for them."

"Why, what has happened to you, Einhard?" Carl asked, laughing. "You are not usually so chary of speaking out!"

Indeed they always teased Einhard for his ready tongue and wondered how he had ever been so shy a lad that it had been difficult to get two words together out of him.

"Send for the envoys," the King said, cutting short Carl's laughter. "There is no need for delay. Bring them immediately."

Within the hour he had heard the tidings that the envoys brought from the imperial court in Byzantium.

The story was like some terrible echo of the degenerate days of Rome, or of the Dark Ages when the Merovingian kings had slaughtered and ravaged their way through Europe, to be put down at last by King Charles's own grandfather, Charles the Hammer.

The days of regency had given the Empress Irene a love of power which she could not bear to relinquish. The young Emperor Constantine, the envoys hastened to explain, had seemed ill-fitted for government. They did not add what the world already knew, that his mother had kept him in submission and neglected his education until he was in fact little better than a witless boy when he came to the throne.

What the envoys had to tell was this: that the

Empress had deposed her son and now reigned in his place.

But this bald fact was not what had sickened Einhard. The further truth emerged gradually, the envoys endeavoring to put a gloss upon the matter to excuse the Empress who had so treated her own son. It had been entirely for his own good, the envoys implied, that the Empress Irene had had her son blinded and sent as a prisoner to a convenient monastery.

Then the envoys hastened to say that the Empress herself had not intended the mutilation, her orders were misunderstood—some enemy of the young Emperor had in fact been responsible. . . .

"To this monster," the King said when the envoys had been coldly dismissed, "I might have delivered my Rhotrud. . . ."

"I am thinking of other things," said Carl. Rhotrud's broken betrothal to Constantine was ancient history and no longer worth speaking about. But there was indeed something more, something immensely important that emerged from this story with such force it seemed to strike Carl a great blow upon the brow. He looked at his father and steeled himself to be bold as he had never been before. It was time for him to speak again the word that Alcuin had used.

"I am thinking," he said, "that the Empress cannot legally sit on the imperial throne. I am thinking that it is she who should be deposed and another crowned in her place. An Emperor, my lord. The Emperor Charles?"

In the silence that followed he wondered if he had

been too bold. The King did not look at him but sat brooding, and over the rest who were there a hush, so expectant that it seemed entirely breathless, hung like some spell.

When at last the King stirred it was with a sharp, dismissive movement. His hand touched Carl's, then pushed him gently away. He gave a slight, soft laugh.

"This lad is after my place already," he said lightly. "If you make me Emperor, Carl, beware of what you do to yourself. For you will be King of the Franks then."

Carl laughed in his turn. The moment which had seemed taut with expectation and even danger slid safely by. But Carl would remember it—the moment when it had seemed certain at last that the dream would become a reality.

XII

The Pope in Peril

DURING THE YEAR that followed the news of Irene's seizure of the imperial throne, Carl found himself increasingly his father's deputy. Saxon affairs were entirely in his hands that spring, and he traveled further than he had ever traveled before. He crossed

the river Elbe into that part of Europe called Nordal-
bingia, and there he set up his court and proceeded
along the familiar lines laid down by his father. There
were further transportations of families and village
communities into new areas where they were obliged
to settle. The outcry against this policy was loud and
bitter, and indeed it brought great hardship. But it was
a measure that had already proved fruitful, separating
troublemakers from their supporters, bringing new
blood to old strains and breaking up the demarca-
tions of tribe and race so that the foundations were
laid of a new society, not Frankish, not Saxon, not
Allemanian or Neustrian—but European.

Then, toward the end of the summer, Carl turned
for home once more, making for Paderborn where
his father was at this time settled.

On any day that Carl turned his horse's head for
home his heart inevitably lightened. Yet full delight
in this particular home-coming was checked by the
knowledge that many stiff problems lay ahead.

There was the personal worry of Queen Liutgarda's
sadly failing health. Above all, there was the matter
that concerned Pope Leo.

Out of a clear sky the previous April, a crisis in
Rome had come as shattering news to the Frankish
court. In its way, it was this crisis that had been responsible for Carl's most recent employment. The news
that had reached Charles the Great had made it clear
to him that he might very shortly be obliged to make
the long journey to Rome. Before he went, he must
be sure his house was in good order. So to the four

quarters of his immense territories he sent his counts and generals to investigate any brewing troubles and set things to rights.

"It may be the Pope will reach Paderborn before us," Carl said to Roriko, who was riding as usual at his right hand. He frowned as he spoke. "I have wondered if my father has not been harsh."

"Best not to question the King's wisdom," Roriko replied. "He cannot forget Pope Hadrian, his dear friend. Pope Leo seems a stranger, for all his great office. And the Queen's health has not made it easy for the King to journey far."

"Should he not have gone to the Pope, Roriko, whatever the circumstances? Was it not altogether churlish to invite the Pope to make the journey? It is long and hard for an injured man."

These were queries which Carl had tried to keep at bay.

In Rome in April the Pope had set out to perform the ceremony known as the Greater Litany, which asked a blessing on the young corn. On the steps of the church of St. Laurence in Lucina he had been violently set upon.

Without the least hint of what was to come, the unsuspecting Pope had found himself cut off from his own court. Armed groups had dispersed the procession which scattered in terror at the assault. Two men, actually of the papal court, Paschalis and Campulus, had fallen upon Leo, thrown him to the ground, and attempted to pluck out his eyes and his tongue.

Some said that the terrible attempt had failed; others

claimed that it had in fact succeeded but that the Pope's sight and speech had been miraculously restored.

The conspirators had dragged the Pope, practically insensible, to the monastery of St. Erasmus. From there he had contrived to escape to St. Peter's. Then it was that one of King Charles's ministers, the Duke of Spoletum, in Rome on state affairs, made contact with the Pope and contrived to spirit away the injured and unhappy man to his own fortress home. From there the duke sent urgent messages to the King of the Franks, asking for immediate help.

The physical attack itself, on such a man, was shocking enough. But it was followed by wild and frightful accusations against Pope Leo. He was charged with every fault which could make him appear unworthy of his great and holy office. The messages he sent to Charles left no doubt as to his expectations.

And the King of the Franks, Charles the Great, had paused before replying.

Could it be that his great ambition stirred in him now so mightily that he took advantage of his position of strength? Did he in fact intend to make the Pope still more his suppliant?

In any event, he had not called up his armies; he had not swept at their head over the Alps and plunged down across the great Lombardy plain seeking vengeance. Instead, he had sent a message of condolence. He had invited the Pope to come to him at Paderborn. There, he had said, they might best be able to discuss these weighty matters and their solution—away from the factions and the scandal that were splitting Roman opinion since the crisis. . . .

The first thing Carl heard when he arrived home was how great and glorious a welcome Pope Leo had received at Paderborn, how the King had heaped on him every honor and consideration and deference. A feeling of warm relief stirred in Carl at this news.

"His Holiness is twice the man he was when he first came," Rhotrud said. "Then he was like a ghost. A poor scarred ghost, Carl. Einhard wept to see him."

"They are together privately for long hours," Bertha put in. "None knows what they speak of, he and the King. . . . Do you remember when we first saw Pope Hadrian on the road before Rome? How surprised we were that he had no wings and no halo!"

Rhotrud smiled. "Yes. I remember."

"It was the same with Pope Leo. He seemed like some poor little chaplain whose enemies had beaten him. But now he has become the Pope again, his great office is like a cloak he has recovered and wrapped round him."

"How long will he be here?" Carl wondered. He gave a sudden boyish guffaw: "Poor Lewis! What he would give to have the Pope under his roof!"

"He must endure without!" Bertha cried. "It is we—the bedizened, the luxurious ones—who have the blessing this time!"

It was a matter of weeks before a plan was agreed upon between the King and the Pope. Yet in that time they must surely have discussed more than the best means of reinstating the Pope? None knew, for the two men talked alone; not even Einhard was admitted. What further plans were laid, Carl wondered, than the simple one for sending Pope Leo back to Rome with commissioners from the King to support him and see justice done?

On a Sunday in October, after celebrating High Mass for the King and his court, Pope Leo rode away from Paderborn. With him went the Archbishop of Cologne and the Archbishop of Salzburg, with five bishops and three counts; of these Bishop Jesse of Amiens and the Count Helmgaud were particularly held in honor by the King.

They rode out into sunshine touched with the sharpness of autumn, a long imposing train of fine men escorting the rightful and elected head of the Church. They went armed and supported by the enormous strength and prestige of that other great ruler, to whom they owed their civil allegiance. With them rode the usual armed escort, the baggage train of mules and pack horses, all the paraphernalia necessary for a journey that would take them several weeks and must include a crossing of the Alps, where the first snows would be piling up over the pass.

As the King watched them go he was watched in his turn, but not even Carl knew at that moment what his father was thinking. Perhaps only that it had been in his power to help the Sovereign Pontiff and he was humbly grateful for the opportunity. But perhaps, more frailly and more humanly, he thought it

was not such a bad thing that Rome should see the
return of Pope Leo supported by the unquestioned
might of Charles the Great, King of the Franks. Or,
deeper still could have been the certainty that now
he had come to the aid of Leo and intended to see
him reinstated, the Pope might be expected to remember how much he owed to his good friend Charles.

Perhaps it was indeed this last consideration that
moved the King. For all at once a strange expression
that was almost sorrow crossed his proud face. He
turned, and as those who had crowded to see the
Pope leave fell back to let him by, the King put one
hand before his eyes. He went swiftly from the palace to the chapel, and there remained for several hours;
until vespers had been sung and the chapel was quiet
again he remained on his knees.

Only then did he uncover his face and rise and
return to the palace.

With the new year came the new century. It was
eight hundred years since the birth of Christ. European civilization was well past its infancy. Christianity, which had been its cradle, must now become its
armor. And for its incorruptible guide one man alone
seemed destined.

In Rome, Pope Leo III was restored to his throne.
But the sensation that events were building up to a
mighty climax remained with the Frankish court. The
King was like a man about to embark upon a greater
journey than the physical journey to Rome. There was

a general surveying of the political scene, a tightening of decrees, a sending out of minor expeditions and embassies, a receiving of new allegiances.

Through all this time of preparation and strange unnamed suspense, the King's concern for his wife remained to plague him. Liutgarda, who had made him happier than he had been since the loss of Hildegarde, seemed daily to fade and dwindle. The physicians were unable to predict her recovery, though she rallied at times so excellently as to seem quite well. But these spells did not last long.

In the spring the King decided he and Liutgarda should make the pilgrimage to the great shrine of St. Martin at Tours, there to pray for her recovery. Not hesitating to make practical use of the journey too, he sent out his messengers to convene a great conference at Tours. Lewis would come from Aquitaine and Pepin from Italy; Anghilbert would be summoned from St. Riquier, and there would be many other men of note and power, trusted deputies of their King, come to counsel with him.

Best of all, King Charles would be able to talk with his sadly missed friend Alcuin, who in the last resort would counsel him how to resolve the problem which absorbed him.

What the men of legal mind had to dispute about was now no secret; they would discuss the validity of Irene's situation as self-styled Empress.

The King and his suite were lodged in the bishop's palace. There, through the warm soft days of spring and early summer, Liutgarda lay quietly. Or she would be carried in a cushioned litter to pray at the shrine of the saint. Her dearest and most devoted attendant was young Himiltrude, Fastrada's daughter, so unlike her mother in her gentleness that it was hard to remember whose child she was.

"She is a little stronger today," Himiltrude would say firmly to the constant inquiries about the Queen's health. "She has eaten more. She has slept better. St. Martin will see her cured and we shall all go happily home to Aachen."

But however hard Himiltrude endeavored to persuade herself and all the rest, most of them knew that Liutgarda was dying, that only a miracle could save her now.

"And I think," she said one day to Carl and Pepin, as they stood rather awkwardly at her bedside, "I think I am not sufficiently blessed for that."

Alcuin came often to sit with Liutgarda. Though they were tinged with the melancholy of coming parting, these days were in fact days when the family could be quietly happy together. They would gather round Liutgarda and listen to Alcuin as they had listened to him during their days at school. Now as then he spoke to them of Bede, of St. Benedict and St. Augustine and all the years of struggle that now lay behind the Church. So many long and difficult years between, yet when Alcuin spoke he did so with such vividness that the birth and death and resurrection of Christ seemed to have happened only yesterday. He told them of the early Fathers, struggling in the desert; of St. Jerome who had the power and the skill to make even wild beasts the willing servants of God. He told of St. Ursula, of St. Catherine and St. Barbara, and all those saints whose names made up what men would come to call the Golden Legend.

Beyond the walls of the palace the increasing summer lay upon the countryside. Liutgarda lingered in that pleasant place as though she could not bear to say good-by to it.

"But I am far from home," she said one day.

They spoke of her words later, Himiltrude and the others.

"What did she mean? That she is still far from Heaven?"

"Or from Aachen, which is our best home on this earth?"

"Or from her birthplace in Allemania, which is many weary miles away?"

On the first day of June, Liutgarda was taken to the shrine of St. Martin. All the family went with her, together with Alcuin, with Anghilbert and with Roriko of Maine, who was now looked upon as one of them. Lewis's wife, Irmingarde, was there too, and chose to take with her their eldest son, now just three years old. Then Bertha decided that her son, too, should go with them. Hartnidus was ten, already a miniature of his father Anghilbert, and a great favorite with Liutgarda. He walked beside her litter holding her hand, which was so white and thin it had the texture of some frail leaf or petal; the boy frequently turned to look at the Queen with an air of anxiety that seemed to add years to his age.

That night Liutgarda asked for the two children. She touched their cheeks and praised their good manners.

"I am better this evening," she declared. "I am stronger. Who knows—perhaps our good St. Martin listened more attentively to young voices—and now makes intercession for me in Heaven!"

But in the morning she lay quietly in her bed, neither moving nor speaking. So she remained until the fourth day of the month, when she died as unobtrusively as she had lived.

"Now," said the King to Carl, "I am an old man. There is no more comfort for me. I am alone indeed."

He put his arm across Carl's shoulders and seemed for a moment to lean upon him as heavily as if he were truly the old infirm and unhappy man he believed himself to be. He had enjoyed only six years of Liutgarda's loving companionship.

The King gave his dead wife a magnificent burial. In chanting procession the monks of Tours escorted the dead Queen by torchlight through the streets of the city to her grave. There were heaped many splendid tokens, and there the King took his final, sad farewell.

"This has aged him," Lewis said to Carl and Pepin. "Now he knows he is an old man and must husband his resources. It is a lesson he is due to learn."

"Old?" Pepin cried. "He will never be old! He will live forever!"

"And that is blasphemy," said Lewis sharply.

Carl frowned at the inevitable, humorless reply to Pepin's extravagance.

"He is an old man today, perhaps," he said. "But tomorrow or the next day—or whenever the horn sounds—he will be himself again. He needs a challenge to answer."

It was as though Carl had foreknowledge of the messengers even then approaching Tours. His sympathy with his father was greater than it had ever been. He not only knew what he wanted for him—as Alcuin, for example, knew—but he was aware that certain tidings were needed to set the King in action once more. Such tidings could lead only to one certain culmination.

In the late afternoon of the same day that the brothers had spoken together, the King sent for Carl. The messengers Carl had hoped might come had reached Tours at noon, and now brought to the King from Rome the only news that could have stirred him from his apathy.

"The Pope is reinstated," he told Carl. "But still there are evil murmurings. He asks my help. It is absolutely necessary that I make the journey to Rome—and with little delay."

"I am glad that you will go," Carl replied.

"And you too," the King said. "You are to come with me."

Carl's heart leaped as it had done when he was a child and his father singled him out for preference.

"When, my lord?"

"We leave at once for Aachen. There are plans to be made. I shall hold a general convention at Mainz. From there, we are headed for Rome. Much may come of this—or little. I say this to you, my son, because if this is the moment toward which I have been striving for so long—then your life, too, must change."

"I understand," Carl said steadily. "And I believe that much will come of it."

The King said no more. Alcuin was coming toward them and it was plain that he had heard the news.

Alcuin was the first, Carl thought, to call him *Emperor*. . . . He knew with certainty that he would not be the last.

XIII

Christmas, A.D. 800

THEY WERE crossing the Alps in winter, struggling in deep snow over tracks which the years of Carl's life had done nothing to improve. Here was the Jupitersberg, here the mound of stones raised to a pagan god, stones which would one day be scattered. Here by the outcrop that made good shelter they pitched their camp by long custom. Once there had been a tent of skins raised to shelter a dearly loved wife and her children; now only soldiers and kings made the journey, and campfires and cloaks sufficed.

It seemed to Carl that he was catching up with his childhood and at the same time passing it forever. Pepin came this way often enough—he was only a week or two ahead of them now. But he had been too young that first time they crossed the mountains to remember anything of what had happened. So in the years that followed he would have gone that way without any memories to tantalize him.

Carl wondered if his father thought about the time they had all camped there together for the night. Did he think about his dear Hildegarde, so long lost to him? Or of Gobbo, whose disinheritance had brought him to disaster, whose name was never spoken now? Did he remember the conflict of mind in which he himself had paced these snows, aware of a terrible decision he had already taken, knowing that he was to split up the family he loved and bring sorrow to his wife?

"Do you remember, Father?" Carl asked at last, as they sat together by the fire. "How we came this way —and you told me I should be your heir?"

"I remember everything," the King replied.

The flames from the campfire painted his great beard, now white as his hair was white, though he was not yet sixty, and shone in his eyes which retained their piercing blue. For him this place was a beginning and an end. Here he had finally steeled himself to his course and from that moment had sprung the whole complex pattern of his future. Then he had not known for certain how the pattern might develop, what shapes, what colors, what textures he might find there. But now he knew. He saw it all; it was bright in color, magnificent in texture, splendid in design—and wanting only a final touch of gold to bring it to perfection. The gold he looked for was the gold of the imperial crown. . . .

Once over the Alps, the King took the great Roman road that led eastward to Ravenna. He had marched all this way with an army at his back and at Ravenna they waited for Pepin to arrive and take over the military command. It was not in any conquering or warlike guise that Charles the Great would enter Rome. Once Pepin was in command, they turned south and rode all together toward Ancona.

At Ancona the King detached his own personal escort from the body of the force, and took the old Flaminian Way that led direct to Rome.

Carl was sorry to see the back of Pepin, who seemed to him to wear a slightly mocking air—as though he saw through all his father's strategy and laughed, though fondly, at its solemnity. As they rode on down the great highway toward the capital, Carl knew again the old loneliness. Einhard was there, but he was always the King's man before all else. Roriko had been left behind; that had been a sad mistake. The men who attended Carl were all trusted and well-liked companions but none was the close friend he needed.

The weather was cold but clear with a fine thin sunshine that at noon strengthened and was warm about the heads and shoulders of the riders. It was the twenty-third of November. That day they came to Nomentum, a few miles short of Rome. Pope Leo rode out to meet them.

"As Hadrian did," the King murmured.

But he did not greet Leo with the humility he had accorded Hadrian. He sat his horse until the Pope came near, then spurred forward to salute him. Only when the Pope had dismounted did the King, too, get out of the saddle. He knelt and kissed the great ring on the hand held out to him. The hand very slightly trembled.

Pope Leo embraced the King of the Franks.

"You are welcome here, my son. God keep you all your days. We have long waited to see you enter Rome."

As Carl in his turn dropped on his knee, he tried to recall the dead Hadrian. But the memory was dim. For him this was neither Leo nor Hadrian, neither one man nor the other, but the Holy Father whose temper and affections need not be measured.

They went into the town and dined at the house of the mayor. King and Pope conferred long and earnestly together, as they had already done at Paderborn. And again none was present; even Einhard was excluded and so could not record what took place, as he recorded so much about the King.

In the early afternoon the Pope left Nomentum and returned to Rome.

"Are we to remain here?" Carl asked, confused by this turn of events.

"Tomorrow," the King answered. "Tomorrow we enter the city. Unarmed. We are no Caesar—no Constantine. Unarmed, Carl. Remember."

Thus, the following morning, they made their entry, a long imposing column of men carrying no weapons. There were crowds in the street to see them. At first these crowds were silent, but gradually feeling warmed, and there were cries, increasing cries of acclamation.

The King rode bareheaded, his back as straight as a sword, his white hair and beard flowing in the light chill breeze, shining like snow in the winter sunshine. Thus they progressed without undue speed toward the basilica of St. Peter.

Einhard spoke sharply and joyously to Carl, who was riding a little short of his father's right hand: "The Pope himself is on the steps of St. Peter's! Look there, Lord Carl—His Holiness is holding out his hands in welcome!"

As the King came to the foot of the steps and dismounted, the Pope held out his arms. Behind him in rank upon rank, the cardinals and bishops and all the clergy of the city of Rome stood waiting. As the King put his foot on the first step and mounted to receive the Pope's embrace, choirs broke forth into loud and joyous psalms.

Thus the Pope and the King of the Franks, followed by the nobles and soldiers who had ridden with him, entered hand in hand into the sanctuary of the blessed Apostle St. Peter. The chanting voices swelled into loud and ever louder praise as the company passed through from the sunlight into the church and the high doors closed behind them.

In the sudden ensuing silence there ran over the assembled crowd in the square below a huge sigh of relief, of relaxation.

The first act of this great drama had been brought to its successful conclusion.

On Christmas Day they were to attend Pontifical High Mass at St. Peter's.

They had been in Rome for a month and a day. In that time the King of the Franks had acted wisely, calmly, strongly. He had sat in judgment on those who had conspired against the Pope. Then that the reinstatement of Leo might be complete and scandal at an end, the King urged him to make a public oath of innocence, denying the charges leveled against him by his enemies. This Pope Leo did, according to the processes of the law. Confidence restored, his people acclaimed him with love, they wept at their recent doubts of him. The matter, after that, could be forgotten.

That had not been the end, however, of the display of the power and glory of King Charles the Great. On the very same day that he sat in judgment, envoys arrived from the Patriarch of Jerusalem, carrying to the King for his safekeeping the keys of the Holy Sepulchre.

By the time Christmas Day arrived there was not a man or a woman in Rome, not a monk or a priest or a civil official who had not realized this: that there resided just then in their city as great a man as any living in the world at that time. And their excitement grew as the tales of his magnificence spread, as they learned of his valor and his piety and his love of scholarship. Added to the fervor and exaltation of the holy season was the expectation of some immediate event great enough to celebrate the occasion. . . .

On Christmas morning Carl went to the King's quarters and found him dressed in the toga and sandals of a Roman patrician.

"I have done this for Pope Leo," he said at once. "It is not my choice."

Carl looked at his father in love and admiration.

"You have never looked more splendid!" he said. "More than a King! An Emperor!"

The King said: "We have argued this long, privately and in counsel, as you know well. It is agreed by all that Irene of Byzantium has seized the throne wrongfully. She has no right of law or heredity. Therefore that throne is vacant. Then what right have I to gain it? Understand this, my son—if I am indeed to be Emperor, I must be so by the choice of the people, not by the favor of the Pope. This I have sworn."

Carl seemed to hear then that ring of iron which was the core of the King. A sudden doubt that his father's purpose could after all be achieved struck at his thoughts and made him shudder as if he had stepped out into a blast of winter wind.

Then Einhard was at the door and it was time to go.

They went in procession to St. Peter's. The Frankish counts and followers of the King were gaily and splendidly dressed. Ahead of them strode the King himself, taller than any, the folds of his toga flowing back from his straight, soldierly limbs.

Once again, the Pope awaited the King in the porch. Once again they entered the basilica together, with the ranks of the King's followers falling in behind, while the clergy and the choirs broke from the supporting mass of men behind the Pope to take up their places for the ceremony.

This time the doors were left open. Those of the crowd who could not squeeze inside, flowed out over the steps and into the open space beyond.

The great church was bright with light and color. The columns and arches, rising one on the other, stretching down the length of the nave, took both light and color to themselves. The mosaics and the tapestries, the gilded figures, the marble ornaments glittered like the very core of magnificence in the light from the enormous cross that carried more than a thousand candles. The swelling sound of the choir was backed by the rustling of vestments and ceremonial garments, the murmur and swish of feet slowly moving on marble as the enormous congregation found places and stood waiting for the moment when the King would make his genuflection before the High Altar with its great canopy and splendor of lights.

The Pope led the King toward the sanctuary steps, almost to the spot beneath which lay the tomb of the Apostle.

Carl watched his father tensely and with a feeling that was half awe and half sorrow. He knew that the climax was upon them but he did not know in what guise it might come. Once before he had knelt in Rome and watched the Pope moving about the altar. . . .

As the memory came to him, Carl saw the King go down on his knees. His hands were folded and his eyes were closed. But Carl, looking to the altar as he had done when he was still a boy, saw again what he had seen there then—not two small crowns to set upon the heads of children, but the great gold crown of Imperial Rome, glittering and shining with a concentration of splendor.

Now the King, his eyes covered, bent his head. The Pope turned with a quick swish of his stiff encrusted vestments, took the crown in both hands and raised it high above the head of the King.

With difficulty Carl checked a cry of warning. What he had instinctively expected had happened in fact. The Pope had retained his ascendancy. . . . As he realized this, Carl realized too that what was taking place was just and right. To complete his purpose, to become the Holy Roman Emperor long dreamed of, the King must yet know himself capable of humility. . . .

A sharp, hissing breath from the excited congregation caused the King to raise his head. He saw the crown in the Pope's hands. He saw the almost tender smile on the Pope's lips as he advanced. For a second, Charles's impulse was to rise and dash the crown away from him.

In those few seconds a dreadful conflict filled him. He knew that at the last, for all his diplomatic skill and cunning statesmanship, he was obliged to give in. He was obliged to accept the fact that the spiritual power had triumphed over the temporal, that he was receiving an honor, not claiming a right. The sacred trust he had so long striven for was to be his—but as a trust indeed and not as a conquest.

The King felt the coldness and the dreadful weight of the crown against his brow and he capitulated, not only in body but in soul. A quick deep shame touched him and left him cold with remorse. He remembered an old prayer, too readily set aside these several years: *Save me, O Lord, from my own arrogance. . . .*

As the crown settled on his head, as the Pope stepped back and raised his hand in blessing, Charles closed his eyes and folded his hands. He stayed thus for perhaps a minute; then he rose.

Instantly a mighty shout burst forth: "Long life and victory to Charles, the most pious Augustus, by God crowned the great and pacific Emperor of the Romans!"

Over and over again the shouts rang to the roof, echoing and beating against the walls, against the columns and the arches, making the candles flicker and flare with the breath of so many voices. The cry was handed back by those pressed in the doorway, carried back and out into the space beyond, so that it seemed all Rome at that moment rang with acclamation.

Was not this all that he could have wished for from the people?

He turned and faced them all. At once they were still. They gazed toward him eagerly.

When the silence was absolute, he spoke.

His voice was as light and yet as carrying as ever. He stood straight and splendid in his toga and the crown glittered on his head.

"I, Charles, Emperor—engage and promise in the name of Christ, in the presence of God and St. Peter the Apostle, to protect and defend the Holy Roman Church in all things profitable to the same, and, God being my helper, to the best of my knowledge and ability."

He said no more. Again the cries of approval and good will deafened him. Then choir and clergy alike broke out into the hymns of thanksgiving that must mark a coronation. And while the singing soared in the splendid building, the Pope, according to accepted custom and tradition, made his own homage to the Emperor. . . .

It was not until Mass was over and they turned to leave the basilica that the Emperor looked toward Carl his son, now King of the Franks. Between the two of them there passed a long deep glance of affection and understanding. However the actual acceptance of the crown had come about, this was the moment toward which father and son and all who moved about them had been traveling for many years.

They stood at the beginning of a new era, of new power and splendor for the Church.

For the greatest ruler the world had yet seen was vowed to the service and protection of the Holy Roman Empire, and he was a man who never faltered.

Author Profile

BARBARA WILLARD (1909-1994) was born in Sussex, England. She enjoyed over fifty years of writing for both children and adults. Her father was an actor, and she made her first stage appearance at the age of eleven. After completion of her formal schooling, she continued acting, and in addition, began writing film scripts and novels for adults. In the late 1950's Miss Willard turned to writing for children, fulfilling a life-long desire. Her favorite genre was historical fiction, of which *Son of Charlemagne* is an early example. Since she had been an only child until the age of twelve, many of her nearly sixty works reflect a fascination with large families. Of her later work, her personal favorites were the acclaimed Mantlemass series, which follow an English country family from the 1400's through 1600's.

Son of Charlemagne was originally published by Doubleday in its Clarion Books series—a special set of titles written to present significant historical times and events from a Christian perspective. Miss Willard also wrote *Augustine Came to Kent* and *If All the Swords in England* for this series.